CHILD MANAGEMENT IN THE PRIMARY SCHOOL

Unwin Education Books

Education Since 1800 IVOR MORRISH
Physical Education for Teaching BARBARA CHURCHER
Organising and Integrating the First School Day JOY TAYLOR
The Philosophy of Education: An Introduction HARRY SCHOFIELD
Assessment and Testing: An Introduction HARRY SCHOFIELD
Education: Its Nature and Purpose M. V. C. JEFFREYS
Learning in the Primary School KENNETH HASLAM
The Sociology of Education: An Introduction IVOR MORRISH
Developing a Curriculum AUDREY and HOWARD NICHOLLS
Teacher Education and Cultural Change H. DUDLEY PLUNKETT and JAMES LYNCH
Reading and Writing in the First School JOY TAYLOR
Approaches to Drama DAVID A. MALE
Aspects of Learning BRIAN O'CONNELL
Focus on Meaning JOAN TOUGH
Moral Education WILLIAM KAY
Concepts in Primary Education JOHN E. SADLER
Moral Philosophy for Education ROBIN BARROW
Principles of Classroom Learning and Perception RICHARD J. MUELLER
Education and the Community ERIC MIDWINTER
Creative Teaching AUDREY and HOWARD NICHOLLS
The Preachers of Culture MARGARET MATHIESON
Mental Handicap: An Introduction DAVID EDEN
Aspects of Educational Change IVOR MORRISH
Beyond Initial Reading JOHN POTTS
The Foundations of Maths in the Infant School JOY TAYLOR
Common Sense and the Curriculum ROBIN BARROW
The Second 'R' WILLIAM HARPIN
The Diploma Disease RONALD DORE
The Development of Meaning JOAN TOUGH
The Place of Commonsense in Educational Thought LIONEL ELVIN
Language in Teaching and Learning HAZEL FRANCIS
Patterns of Education in the British Isles NIGEL GRANT and ROBERT BELL
Philosophical Foundations for the Curriculum ALLEN BRENT
World Faiths in Education W. OWEN COLE
Classroom Language: What Sort? JILL RICHARDS
Philosophy and Human Movement DAVID BEST
Secondary Schools and the Welfare Network DAPHNE JOHNSON *et al.*
Educating Adolescent Girls E. M. CHANDLER
Classroom Observation of Primary School Children RICHARD W. MILLS
Essays on Educators R. S. PETERS
Comparative Education: Some Considerations of Method BRIAN HOLMES
Education and the Individual BRENDA COHEN
Moral Development and Moral Education R. S. PETERS
In-Service Education within the School ROLAND W. MORANT
Learning to Read HAZEL FRANCIS
Children and Schooling PHILIP GAMMAGE
Relating to Learning PETER KUTNICK
The Foundations of Morality JOEL J. KUPPERMAN
Child Management in the Primary School TESSA ROBERTS
Managing Educational Innovations AUDREY NICHOLLS
Paradigms and Language Games DAVID STENHOUSE
The Libertarians and Education MICHAEL P. SMITH

Child Management in the Primary School

TESSA ROBERTS

Department of Education, University of Manchester

London
GEORGE ALLEN & UNWIN
Boston Sydney

**George Allen & Unwin (Publishers) Ltd,
40 Museum Street, London WC1A 1LU, UK**

George Allen & Unwin (Publishers) Ltd,
Park Lane, Hemel Hempstead, Herts HP2 4TE, UK

Allen & Unwin, Inc.,
9 Winchester Terrace, Winchester, Mass. 01890, USA

George Allen & Unwin Australia Pty Ltd,
8 Napier Street, North Sydney, NSW 2060, Australia

First published in 1983

British Library Cataloguing in Publication Data

Roberts, Tessa.
Child management in the primary school.
1. Classroom management
2. Elementary schools – England
I. Title
372.11′2′07 LB3013
ISBN 0-04-370126-4
ISBN 0-04-370127-2 Pbk

Library of Congress Cataloging in Publication Data

Roberts, Tessa.
Child management in the primary school.
Includes bibliographical references and index.
1. Classroom management. 2. Elementary school teaching. I. Title.
LB3013.R55 1983 372.11′02 83-3706
ISBN 0-04-370126-4
ISBN 0-04-370127-2 (pbk.)

Typeset in 10 on 11 point Times by Typesetters (Birmingham) Ltd
and printed in Great Britain
by Biddles Ltd, Guildford, Surrey

Contents

Chapter 1

Introduction

A book about managing children rests on the assumption that it is proper that children should be managed by the teachers who teach them. Most adults who work in primary schools and most parents would probably believe this to be so, but the general acceptance of an idea should not protect it from critical scrutiny. Before we enter into any discussion of ways and means of managing children effectively, we should be quite sure that it is right for us to do so. What might be the grounds for objection?

Child-centred theorists could be unhappy about notions of child management. With their benign view of the nature of the child, they would tend to see dangers in control of children which might pervert the natural course of their development. Rousseau (1911), for example, suggests that 'nature provides for the child's growth in her own fashion and this should never be thwarted' (p. 50), and the pages of Pestalozzi and Froebel abound with references to trees, branches, seeds and flowers which picture the responsibility of the teacher as that of ensuring that growing conditions are not adverse and refraining from taking action which might distort the natural line of growth. Positive child management might well prove an unacceptable concept to anyone strongly committed to such a view, and if confined and inhibited behaviour were either the intention or the outcome, then child management would indeed be a very suspect notion.

Those who regard education from a Marxist perspective might be even more dubious about the concept. Writers such as Bowles and Gintis (1976) see the American education system as operating largely in order to preserve the status quo in society so that the workers know their place and keep to it. Personal development is limited to 'forms compatible with submission to authority' (p. 266). Is our own system any different? Evidently not. Sharp and Green (1975) have described how they see this process of social control beginning in the very early days of the infant school where the 'normal pupil' is the one who understands and accepts the teacher's working system while the 'maladjusted' child is the one who either does not understand or does not conform. Corrigan (1979) offers the pupils' picture of a similar process at work years later in two secondary schools. By this time, many of the pupils are totally alienated, seeing their teachers as members of a different culture who exert a power over them which they resent. If child management were simply to involve more effective means of subordinating children for society's purposes then many teachers would quite rightly have grave misgivings about it.

The child-centred theorists and the Marxists alert us to very real dangers, but what we are contemplating here are not systems of suppression or distortion but systems of facilitation. One of the soundest arguments for setting up conditions for controlled behaviour in a primary school classroom is that they make it easier for teaching and learning to take place. The Plowden Report (1967), for all its emphasis on children's interests, was in no doubt about this. The kind of active and involved learning which the committee envisaged depended not on 'mere progressiveness' (para. 738) but on the establishing of relationships between teacher and child about which there was 'nothing soft or flabby' (para. 750). They saw standards of civilised behaviour and mutual respect among the children as necessary preconditions for the more informal regimes they were advocating.

Since Plowden, we have had time to give more thought to the other member of the partnership, the teacher, and there is growing evidence (e.g. Dunham, 1977; Kyriacou and Sutcliffe, 1978) to suggest that one of the major sources of the considerable stress that teachers experience today is disruptive behaviour on the part of children. The teacher who is subject to the stress which can be brought about by having to cope with this kind of uncontrolled behaviour is unlikely to be at his most effective.

Beyond this very practical argument that good child management enables both teacher and child to get on with the job, there are more idealistic reasons why teachers should exert control over the way children behave. The first of these is that they have the responsibility of the adult for the immature child who cannot conceivably see what may be in his own best, long-term interests. As Dearden (1976) unequivocally states,

> On the frankly paternalistic ground of being in his best interests, it therefore falls to adults who have a special knowledge of him, and a natural or professional care for him, to try to discover those interests and secure their satisfaction on his behalf. Parents and teachers therefore rightly exercise a certain directive influence over him for his good. (p. 58)

A teacher cannot escape this moral duty to guide the young in his charge.

The second reason is that the way a teacher controls, or fails to control, the class can affect the development of the child's sense of autonomy. One of the teacher's major responsibilities, according to

Entwistle (1970), is to foster self-discipline in the learner. For him, this includes self-control, self-direction, self-reliance and a sense of responsibility. A child is unlikely to make much progress towards this kind of self-discipline if he lives and works in a situation which provides neither models nor experience of control.

In looking at methods of child management, then, we are considering ways of making it easy for the work of the classroom to proceed based on the immediate exercise of the teacher's adult authority but with the prospect of its ultimate redundancy as children become increasingly self-controlled. Before we begin to explore the factors which it may be important to take into account in planning effective strategies, however, it is as well to reassure ourselves that the exercise really is worth the effort. We need to be reassured on two counts: first, that what is done in schools really does make some difference to the children, and second, that there really is a need for more effective planning. If everybody manages without difficulty then the subject needs no investigation.

DO SCHOOLS AND TEACHERS MAKE A DIFFERENCE?

Evidence from surveys such as those produced for the Plowden Committee (e.g. Wiseman, 1967) and the National Child Development Study (Davie *et al.*, 1972) has tended to concentrate attention on factors outside the school which affect children's school performance. One of the results has been a tendency to overlook or even to be pessimistic about the degree of influence that schools themselves can have on the way their children behave. At a common-sense level, teachers know that the way they deal with children makes a difference, for better or for worse, but evidence has been hard to come by. For this reason, Rutter's (1979) findings in relation to children in inner London secondary schools have been professionally cheering. He and his colleagues found that differences in the way a school operated as a social institution and the way teachers behaved towards the pupils were systematically related to differences in the way pupils themselves behaved both in the classroom and outside school. Findings like these give teachers renewed confidence in their power to influence affairs and although they were based on observation of secondary schools, there is no reason to suppose that the situation in primary schools is any different. Indeed, Heal (1978), in a rather smaller study, found that primary schools too were able to exert a positive influence on children. They differed in the degree of misbehaviour occurring among their pupils outside school even allowing for differences in their catchment areas and the personal characteristics of their pupils.

The other side of the picture, of course, is that schools can differ too in the adverse effect they have on their pupils' behaviour both inside and outside school. Burt and Howard (1952) provided evidence thirty years ago that school conditions, most particularly the personal relations established between child and teacher, were among the chief factors associated with maladjusted behaviour amongst pupils, and Hargreaves has long been suggesting (e.g. 1967, 1976) that schools themselves may positively promote delinquency.

HOW EFFECTIVE ARE CURRENT LEVELS OF CHILD MANAGEMENT?

If we were to believe some of the contributors to the Black Papers, we would have an immediate reply to this question, for they see themselves surrounded by schools where *laissez-faire*, permissive attitudes obtain with a resulting decline in standards (Cox and Dyson, 1971). For them, current levels of child management are clearly unsatisfactory. Even in the Green Paper (DES, 1977) it was suggested that the widespread use of a child-centred approach had tended to deteriorate into a lack of order in primary schools.

More dispassionate observation would suggest a different picture, however. In neither of the recent surveys conducted by HMI into primary and secondary schools (DES, 1978, 1979) was a high incidence of behavioural problems noted. On the contrary, the majority of the secondary schools were orderly communities and much of what was going on in primary schools appeared safely dull. It does not seem that we need to fear chaos on the rampage sapping the energy of our schools.

General appearances may be deceptive, however. Work such as that of Dunham and Kyriacou and Sutcliffe suggests that a high price may be being paid for this orderliness in terms of teacher stress. A price may also be being paid in terms of unadventurousness for, contrary to popular belief, HMI did not find widespread progressivism in primary schools but rather an over-concentration on a narrow range of basic skills at the expense of provision for experience – or interest-related learning. In other words, teachers were sticking to things which were useful but organisationally safe. One of the implications must be that many felt insecure at venturing beyond into the kind of activities where more demanding levels of child management would be necessary.

Moreover, whatever the situation for teachers as a whole, there is one group who tend to experience considerable difficulty in managing children satisfactorily. These are the probationers, who need to learn gradually the subtle management skills which many experienced teachers operate intuitively. There is plenty of evidence (e.g. Hannam *et al.*, 1976) to show that whatever kind of school they are working in, this is one of the key areas that teachers in the early stages of their career tend to worry about.

For the inexperienced, for those who cope with difficulty and for those who would like to be more adventurous in their teaching, a study of child management techniques is likely to prove rewarding.

The management of children in primary schools is an extremely complex matter. The teacher's own management style and the steps he takes or avoids taking may appear to constitute the main action but they are only part of an intricate scenario where many less immediately evident factors have a role to play.

Some of these can be grouped together under the general heading of setting. The action does not take place against a featureless background. It occurs at a particular point in time and in a physical environment, usually the classroom but also at times the school or the neighbourhood. Meanwhile the characters are involved in an occupation which is not ostensibly part of the management process but may nevertheless have a considerable effect on the main action. Contextual factors such as these set limits and create possibilities.

The other important feature of the action is the group of characters themselves. Here the teacher is only one of many. There are the children, who are far from passive management material, and other adults such as parents make an appearance from time to time. All those who are part of the scene, however fleetingly, can affect the action either directly or through the pressure of their perceptions of the situation. All have their own view of what happens and their own expectations of what is likely to happen and this in turn can influence the way the action develops. Of no one is this more true than the teacher, who does not act according to a script prepared for him but plans and improvises his own according to his perception of his role and his expectations of others.

If we are to attempt to unravel the complexities of child management, we must examine not only the *style and strategies of management* but also the *setting* and the *people and perceptions* involved.

STYLE AND STRATEGIES

A teacher's style of management and the strategies and techniques that he employs are likely to make a considerable difference to the effectiveness with which he manages the children in his charge. In discussing the topic, it may be useful to distinguish between two aspects of teacher behaviour: the habitual style of control which helps to establish the normal atmosphere of the classroom, and the specific techniques which are employed to deal with incidents that occur.

Probably the most helpful work produced so far on general management techniques is that of Kounin (1970). As a result of extensive analysis of videotapes of primary school classrooms in action, he proposes certain dimensions of management which appear to be associated with work involvement and lack of disruptive behaviour on the part of pupils. These include *withitness* (having eyes in the back of your head), *overlapping* (dealing with more than one thing at a time), *movement management* (keeping things flowing smoothly without losing momentum), *maintaining group focus* (keeping all children involved and accountable), *avoiding satiation* (initiating and maintaining a level of enthusiasm) and *variety* (providing variety of content, presentation, materials, activity, grouping, and so on).

Beneath the transatlantic terminology, Kounin is offering a practically useful description of the kind of managerial style which is geared to reducing the likelihood of trouble. But he found that specific techniques for dealing with trouble when it does arise were difficult to generalise. What worked for one teacher was singularly unsuccessful for another. It may be that he was looking at the wrong level of generality, however. Clearly, there are principles which can be drawn from the way successful teachers deal with troublesome behaviour and a theory which goes some way towards explaining those principles is that of Skinner (1968).

Skinner has built up a learning theory in the behaviourist tradition which means that he is concerned only with what people do, not with their intentions. What they do, he claims, is largely controlled by what follows their doing it; if a pleasurable situation follows, they will be much more likely to repeat that action than if it does not.

Skinner also emphasises the importance of the stimulus situation in which an action occurs. A change in that situation can affect the likelihood of the behaviour occurring: a pigeon may peck for corn but with beads he will remain inactive. A complete method of dealing with disruptive behaviour *(behaviour modification)* has been built up on a combination of Skinner's theories and his experimental methods, and O'Leary and O'Leary (1972) describe its successful operation in a variety of situations. In the main, however, it has been found most useful in small group situations and with grossly disturbed behaviour. The teacher in the ordinary classroom can afford to be more selective in what he takes from Skinner. He can accept what is useful without endorsing Skinner's rejection of motivation and intentions.

The most important thing for him to take may be confidence in his own powers to control difficult behaviour. First of all, since he can influence what follows a child's actions, that is, he can have a hand in the arrangement of what Skinner calls the contingencies, he can expect to be effective in influencing future behaviour. What he must be is subtle and tireless in devising outcomes. It is not always the most obvious reinforcement that works best. Secondly, he may look for ways of changing the situation where this behaviour usually occurs if he wants to prevent a repetition of something he regards as undesirable. Bandura (1969) documents a bewildering variety of reinforcers ranging from a nod of the head to electrical stimulation of the brain, and stimuli ranging from the predictable (sight of food for overeating) to the unusual (the national anthem for an attack of asthma).

In educational contexts the range may not be so extreme, but there is still tremendous scope for a teacher to vary both the reinforcement patterns and the stimulus situation obtaining in a classroom in order to bring about a change in the way children behave. In other words, there are positive steps he can take and strategies he can employ which, set within the context of an effective style of management, can give him a great deal of control over the way children behave.

Yet things do not always go as smoothly as might be hoped, for other factors are likely to be involved.

SETTING

One of the most important contributions that sociologists have made to educational thinking is to direct our attention to the fact that nothing happens in a vacuum. Children, like teachers, behave well or badly in a context. To understand and influence that behaviour we need to attend to the setting in which it occurs.

Delamont (1976) suggests that we can conveniently consider setting under four headings: temporal, physical, institutional and educational. The temporal setting involves not only the experience of the teacher and the stage of development of the children but also the point reached in the development of classroom understanding: classroom life is not static but something which changes as shared meaning and understanding is built up during the year.

The physical setting involves the location of the classroom within the school and the location of the school within the community, both of which can have a significant effect on life within the classroom. Probably the aspect to which primary school teachers will tend to pay most positive attention, however, is the third aspect catalogued by Delamont, the layout and decor of the classroom itself. Certainly, this is emphasised in most books on primary school practice (see, for example, Ridgway, 1976) where there is often a particular regard for the decor of the room. The belief that layout can influence an activity was at least the ostensible rationale for open plan schools (DES, 1970), and indeed Nash (1981) has demonstrated that the spatial organisation of a classroom can have a considerable effect on the learning of very young children.

Just how profoundly physical setting may affect the attitudes and behaviour of those who work in a classroom is not always fully appreciated, however. Jackson (1968) was one of the first to explore the implications for classroom life and understanding of apparently superficial features such as available space and equipment. More recently, Hamilton (1977) documents the disturbance caused by what might have appeared a trivial modification to one of the physical features of the classroom: a reduction in the supply of chairs to a new open plan school. The significance of such factors to those concerned evidently extends well beyond their immediate appearance or convenience.

For Delamont, the institutional setting consists of the organisational structure and the official and unofficial policies of the school as a whole. It is true that a classroom cannot exist in isolation but the significance of the institutional background will vary from school to school. A strong organisational structure and coherent policies are more likely to exert influence within the classroom than a poorly planned or *laissez-faire* regime, but while that influence may support progress, as in the successful schools described in Cane and Smithers's (1971) study of reading, it may also be limiting and repressive, as in the Salford elementary school attended by Robert Roberts (1976).

Educational setting is perhaps the most important of all for the primary school teacher who is anxious to avoid behavioural problems in the classroom. Delamont sees the educational setting essentially in terms of the curriculum, including methods, materials and forms of assessment. In some respects, this may seem a strange way of looking at things. What is taught and learned and how this process takes place is generally considered to be the central business of a school (for example, by Blenkin and Kelly, 1981). How then can we appear to demote it to a 'setting' against which interaction takes place?

The change is chiefly one of focus. If we focus on the curriculum, then classroom interaction becomes the setting within which the curriculum operates. If we focus on the way teachers and children behave, then the curriculum becomes a feature of the setting within which people act. But even when regarded as only one aspect of the general setting for teacher/child behaviour, educational setting is of supreme importance in this respect.

King (1978), for example, suggests that the way that learning activities were organised in the infant classrooms he studied made an important contribution to the exercise of social control. Boydell (1978) provides an extensive discussion of the way grouping of children affects the patterns of interaction that take place in primary classrooms. Entwistle (1970) and Connie Rosen (1967) have maintained that it is in the work to be done that teacher and children meet most fruitfully: the work provides the purpose for interaction and it is in this indirect way that relationships are most successfully built. The setting of tasks, the selection of materials, the grouping of children, the allocation of time are all matters of supreme importance in creating good working conditions where all concerned can relate well to each other.

The relative importance of the various aspects of setting discussed by Delamont will vary from school to school and from situation to situation, but it is difficult to envisage any primary school where the way that people behave towards each other is not fundamentally influenced by the physical setting in which they work and the educational setting which determines their normal pattern of activity. These two aspects of setting warrant very serious consideration by teachers who are aiming to improve the effectiveness of their child management policies.

The temporal aspects of setting are much more difficult to isolate since they are but one characteristic of the gradual development of understanding among those who share the same classrooms and are perhaps best considered as a feature of this process.

Institutional setting sets the overall context for the management of children and while, in primary schools, this may not appear to affect substantially the day-to-day action within the classroom, it always remains a potential source of influence which it would be dangerous to leave out of account.

PEOPLE AND PERCEPTIONS

Children's expectations about the way teachers should behave and the criteria which they employ to evaluate them have been investigated quite extensively over the last two decades and excellent reviews of this work can be found in Hargreaves (1972) and in Docking (1980). Although separated by a number of years and therefore by no means relying on the same material, Hargreaves and Docking reach very similar conclusions. They find a remarkable degree of agreement among pupils of all ages and all ability levels about what they expect of the good teacher and what they dislike about the teachers they consider poor. Children universally appear to expect teachers to keep order; a good teacher exerts firm but non-punitive control. The reverse of this is that they dislike the teacher who is too soft with them or is hard in the sense of being overbearing, excessive and indiscriminate in his punishing. Children also like teachers who are effective in getting them to learn something; especially those who can explain subject matter and arrange learning situations in such a way that the children feel that they achieve something. In terms of personality they particularly value friendliness and a sense of humour.

Of course, as Docking points out, just because children have these expectations of teachers this does not mean that teachers should necessarily fulfil them. A teacher may not think it right to exercise the degree of overt control that the children would like, for example, preferring to foster a greater degree of self-control on their part. Nevertheless, a teacher is more likely to be able to change pupils' perceptions of his role if he has first fulfilled their initial requirements. An unacceptable person is likely to have little influence.

Research shows children's expectations about teachers to be on the whole reasonable and sensible. Unfortunately, some teachers appear in a far less flattering light when their expectations about children are examined. They are shown to be influenced by all kinds of superficial characteristics which lead them to make premature judgements about children and then treat them accordingly. Sometimes the judgements appear as overt labels ('fishwife', 'troublemaker') and sometimes the labelling is simply implied in the teacher's attitude. Either way, children tend to perceive these judgements and to respond to this treatment as expected, thus obligingly fulfilling what may have been a false prophecy and vindicating the teacher's judgement.

The judgements involve varying degrees of irrationality. They may be based, for example, on race (e.g. Mabey, 1981), sex (e.g. Hartley, 1978), academic stream (e.g. Hargreaves, 1967), social class (e.g. Rist, 1970), or physical attractiveness (e.g. Clifford and Walster, 1973).

The range of findings is extensive and the depressing results of premature classification are well documented in terms of both children's behaviour (Hargreaves *et al.*, 1975) and children's achievement (Pidgeon, 1970). But clearly this is not the whole of the story. It is just the most dramatic part. If teachers can communicate the expectation of failure and disorderliness in such a way as to make them happen, there must also be great scope for communicating the reverse and making it happen. Indeed, one of the earliest pieces of research in this field, by Rosenthal and Jacobson (1968), claimed to show how teachers could bring about great progress in children when they were falsely led to believe them capable. Unfortunately, the methodology of the study has been questioned and meanwhile researchers have found it a lot more fun to search out the weaknesses of teachers.

But there have been documented successes. Low ability children have done well in French where teachers considered there was no reason why they should not (Burstall, 1970). Boys, usually shown to be poorer readers in the early stages than girls, did as well as girls in classes where teachers believed they could be equally successful (Palardy, 1969). Staines (1958) showed that it is possible for a teacher to improve the way children see themselves by the way he talks to them, the comments he makes and the learning situations he devises.

There is every reason to suppose that teachers who minimise the disadvantages or handicaps that their children may experience, who keep a watchful eye on their own prejudices and who concern themselves with future possibilities, rather than past failures, may help children to achieve higher standards of work and behaviour than would normally be thought probable. Perhaps the most important safeguard is that teachers should have what Peters (1966) termed respect for their children as persons, acknowledging them as distinct individuals with peculiar feelings and purposes incorporating pride and aspirations.

There remains the question of how children see each other. According to Mussen *et al.* (1974), the great task for the child in the primary school in terms of his social development is to move away from dependence on his parents and to gain acceptance by his peer group. When they begin school most children are impervious to pressure from their peers, but as they progress into the junior classes, belonging to the group matters more and more and the tendency to adopt the attitudes and values of peers grows strong. The qualities which make a child acceptable to his peer group are varied and predictable as are those which make him unacceptable. Hartup (1970) provides an extensive discussion of research concerned with the establishment and functioning of peer groups, and Root (1977) offers a sensitive analysis of the way these may affect the individual in the classroom.

Strong as the peer group may be, however, it is not without susceptibility to adult influence. Most work in this area has concerned pupils beyond the primary school age range but, nevertheless, it has been found that adults can manipulate friendship groups (Sherif *et al.*, 1955), affect the social acceptability of individuals (Flanders and Havumaki, 1960) and sway the attitude of the peer group as a whole (Lewin *et al.*, 1939). The teacher who can harness the power of the peer group has a means of extending his own influence and of arranging support for a child who might otherwise be rejected.

Teachers and pupils are the most enduring members of classroom society, but other adults enter the scene from time to time and are inevitably a complicating factor in the situation. While the children may well look for similar relationships with all adults, appreciating generally those qualities they value in teachers (certainly McPhail *et al.* (1972) suggest that this is the case for adolescents), the reverse may not be true. Non-professional adults appear unlikely to perceive children in quite the same way as teachers do. Taylor (1980) suggests that there is an almost inevitable division between the teacher and the parent, for instance, because each has different tasks and responsibilities in relation to the child, the parent being committed to accepting him 'warts and all' and the teacher to an objective judgement, particularly in terms of achievement. Certainly, it seems that there is frequent disagreement between parents and teachers about what constitutes problem behaviour (Shepherd *et al.*, 1971).

This difference in perspective may be one of the reasons why teachers do not always feel comfortable with parents in the classroom and why parents do not always find it easy to participate in school activities. The recent NFER report (Cyster *et al.*, 1981) notes a considerable increase in the degree of parental participation, but a kind of mutual uneasiness still seems to exist between many parents and teachers, particularly where the parents are working class, and this could make a teacher feel less secure in his role as manager.

Richardson (1973) records a similar uneasiness between teachers and those fulfilling what she terms a service role in a school (secretary, caretaker, and so on). The situation in a large secondary school such as she is concerned with and that in a primary school are in many ways quite different, but the nub of the problem appears the same, that of 'boundary control'. Who has a right to ask what of whom? This uncertainty can lead to situations where too much or, more usually in the case of primary schools, too little is asked of those in a service role. The kind of misunderstanding which thus arises can deprive the teacher of a valuable support system or, even worse, constitute a positive handicap in his exercise of control.

Child management is no different from any other kind of personnel management in that an understanding of the people concerned, their attitudes and the relationships among them is crucial for the success of the manager, for many of the problems that are likely to arise in connection with control in the classroom can be either exacerbated or smoothed away by the attitudes and relationships among those involved.

The aim in this chapter has been to provide a lightning tour of some of the work which has contributed to our present understanding of what happens in classrooms. The rest of the book will be devoted to an exploration of how we can use the framework of that understanding to improve our ability to control what goes on. A practical illustration of the issues discussed will be included wherever possible.

The exploration will begin with a consideration of overall class control and the particular measures primary school teachers can take to ensure that the outcomes of children's behaviour are appropriately rewarding or negative.

A consideration of settings will follow, particular emphasis being given to the physical environment constituted by the classroom and the educational environment constituted by what the children do and how they do it.

The major part of the book will be given over to people, however, as the unpredictable sphere of human actions and interactions represents for the teacher at once the greatest source of hazard and the greatest opportunity for success.

Finally, there will be an examination of some of the implications of the institutional context for all this activity, that is, the school itself.

Chapter 2

Developing Class Control

Having day-to-day control of a large group of people is something for which it is difficult to be prepared. It is a situation to which life does not, in the normal way of things, call us. Yet it is important to adapt to the experience quickly for delay in coping with problems of class control tends to feed them and can lead to overwhelming growth.

Even the most experienced teacher will find problems at the beginning of a new school year. They may not show because he has probably developed effective techniques for dealing with them but that does not mean that they are not there. The children are strange to him; he will need to get to know them and learn how to handle them. They will bring with them the conventions of the previous year which may conflict with those which he wishes to establish. He will have to feel his way towards an understanding of their current pattern of achievement so that he can provide work at an appropriate level.

These problems are present for the teacher at the beginning of a new career, too, and for him there are likely to be additional difficulties. In part these are associated with deciding what kind of teacher he wants to be. The new teacher has to interpret for himself his role as group manager and decide upon what sort of group he wants those in his charge to become. But he will also need to develop techniques which will enable him to achieve this.

For all teachers, then, there is development. The control of classes is not something static which is clamped on at the beginning of the year and remains in place until it is removed in July. Rather it is a dynamic, evolving process which teacher and children work out together during the year. For both experienced and inexperienced teachers change will occur through deepening teacher/child knowledge and the gradual establishing of conventions. For the inexperienced teacher, change will also tend to occur with clarification of aims and the development of techniques for handling children.

A discussion of these areas of potential change should fairly start and end with the concerns of the inexperienced teacher, for these will incorporate those of his experienced colleague. It must start with clarification of aims, because the areas of interpersonal knowledge, conventions and techniques can only be sensibly and practically discussed within the context of agreement about an overall aim. It must end with techniques, for it is on the effectiveness of techniques for handling a group of children that the success of the whole enterprise rests.

CLARIFICATION OF AIMS

Experienced teachers are most likely to be already operating according to an overall aim even though this may not be formulated and may simply be to have as peaceful a life as possible. The new teacher has to decide what his most fundamental aim is now that he has joined the profession. At the beginning of the year he may be unsure of what this is, but gradually he will develop a sense of direction and begin to work out the route. Alternatively, he may begin with one very clearly formulated aim but decide to modify this in the light of reality. In either case, some change will most probably occur during the first year of teaching.

For experienced teachers change in this area may be less likely, but circumstances such as inservice opportunities or unfortunate career experiences may yet bring it about.

Discussion of the aims of primary education has tended to concentrate on the distinction between what Ashton *et al.* (1975) have called the *societal* purpose and the *individual* purpose. Those subscribing to the societal purpose would see education as equipping the child with the skills and attitudes which will enable him to make a useful contribution and live harmoniously in society. Those subscribing to the individual purpose would see education as fostering the development of individuality and independent judgement in the child.

Of course we could argue interminably about this, but for most teachers there is little real conflict. As Ashton *et al.* found, most tend to subscribe to some extent to both views, presumably looking towards a child who could both live harmoniously and reserve his independence of judgement. Certainly, this kind of working compromise enables thoughtful teachers to get on with the job.

Much more fundamental is the division between those who are cynical and those who are idealistic in the views they hold, and often this division is associated with experience.

It may be inevitable that teachers become less idealistic as they acquire experience in the classroom, but it is possible to become more realistic without becoming cynical. Where the movement is in the direction of greater cynicism and self-interest, this may well be due to a failure of technique which has prevented the new teacher from putting his aims into practice. Ideals will almost inevitably founder if they are unsupported by effective techniques of control. In such a situation, however, change in the area of techniques rather than ideals is likely to produce a happier outcome for both teacher and children.

INTERPERSONAL KNOWLEDGE AND UNDERSTANDING

At the beginning of a school year, most teachers inherit records of varying degrees of helpfulness. This is where knowledge of the class begins but other teachers' records of the children are soon superseded by a teacher's own experience of them. Increasing knowledge of each child's abilities enables a teacher to provide work which is more precisely geared to his level of achievement.

Aptness of learning tasks and materials is an important factor in the creation of a purposeful working environment where children can function with a degree of independence. At the beginning of the year, a new teacher may take some time to get the measure of what a given age-group may be capable of doing. An experienced teacher may take a little time to adjust from the maturity of the class which has just left him to the comparative rawness of the class which he has just received. A variety of open tasks such as story-writing and sequenced tasks such as computation will provide an idea of the stage children have reached and where they might go next.

Increasing knowledge of each child as an individual should also lead to greater personal understanding through which a child can be taught to value himself. Unfortunately, it is easy for a teacher to give children the impression that he is simply not interested in them as people. This can be conveyed in a variety of ways. Some teachers daily demonstrate to children their lack of importance by rushing into the classroom at the last minute and leaving it the moment the bell rings for playtime or dinner-time. Others reveal the irrelevance of children's work by seldom looking at it, commenting on it, or displaying it. Many suggest that children are of secondary importance by automatically excluding them from adult conversation: an adult visitor occasions adult conversation with the teacher, not general conversation with both teacher and children.

In such ways is it conveyed to a class of children that the teacher lacks interest in them as a group of people. If he spends little time in personal conversation the impression may also be given that he lacks concern for them as individuals.

The interested teacher will talk to them, talk to others about them, think about them. And such an interest will show itself in sensitively varied handling of different children, in the seeking out of materials and experiences likely to appeal to the individual and in the ability to provide background information and insights on any child when required.

There are two dangers to guard against. First, interest might become intrusion. Some children may not wish to share their confidences with their teacher and some may have areas of their experience which they wish to keep private. A teacher should respect such reticence. Indeed, it is respect for the child as having the right to reserve those parts of himself that he wishes and to convey the image that he desires to have of himself that sets the tone for successful communication between teacher and children. It is manifest in the way a teacher speaks both to the class and to individuals. Of course, there are limits. If a child wishes to project himself as a latter-day Genghis Khan, this will adversely affect the self-image of other children around him. Similarly, if a child is inclined to see himself as a failure, this cannot be considered a happy state of affairs. But such instances are rare and for the most part a respect for the child as an interesting but independent individual can be conveyed.

Secondly, interest may lead to indulgence; an awareness of a child's difficulties may lead to a reluctance to make demands upon him so that he does not function at the level of which he is capable. It is quite possible to spend so much time blowing a little girl's nose, combing her hair and pulling up her socks that you never actually get round to listening to her read.

CONVENTIONS

All classes quickly establish conventions even if they are only those of noise and chaos. Since neither independence nor social consideration tend to flower in an atmosphere of chaos where the loudest voice wins the day, it is as well for the teacher to take firm charge of the conventions right from the outset in order to set up conditions favourable to the promotion of good order.

This is chiefly a matter of specifying the limits which will be regarded as tolerable. These limits may operate in any sphere of classroom activity but there are four key areas where the establishment of limits can be considered. These are movement, noise, manner and work production.

MOVEMENT

At certain times of the day a concerted movement by the whole class may be required, as when they leave the room, for example. Here an orderly system is necessary, if only for the sake of general safety.

Most often movement is an individual matter, however, and the conventions which apply to it have far-reaching implications for life and work in the classroom in general. If children never move from their allotted places at all unless requested to do so, the scope for them to accept responsibility for their work is minimal. If, on the other hand, they are allowed to move boisterously around the room to no apparent purpose and with little regard for others, self-indulgence rather than self-control is likely to be the result. A teacher must decide on the degree and the manner of movement that he will allow and then make quite sure that children understand what is acceptable and what is not. Simple criteria for acceptability are movement that has a purpose, movement that does not limit the freedom of others by interrupting what they are doing and movement that would be considered normal in public places. All this implies a careful, purposeful movement about the room by individual children.

NOISE

The noise level in a classroom which teachers find tolerable varies enormously. One may find anything above a murmur objectionable. Another may find nothing wrong in quite a high level of sound. But a teacher's preferences are not really a reasonable criterion here. A class is made up of a large number of individuals of whom the teacher is only one. As with any large group of people, there is likely to be a wide variation in individual preferences. Some more objective criteria have to be sought.

Here, taking effective communication as a yardstick, we might agree that when an individual is speaking to the group as a whole, there should be no noise at all as this inhibits communication. When individuals wish to speak to each other the level of noise should be sufficiently low to enable them to communicate in normal conversational tones; if the convention allows anyone to shout, everyone will have to shout to make himself heard.

MANNER

Manner is a very elusive thing to discuss because the attitude it conveys is often unexpressed. The high speed of personal interaction makes it difficult to pinpoint the things that are expressed without words until after the event. In this way, unacceptable but unspoken comments may be allowed to pass.

One way to guard against this is for the teacher to have a well-fashioned mental template of what is acceptable, against which a child's manner can be instinctively set. This does not mean that he will always react according to a similarly well-fashioned template but simply that when a child's manner might be deemed unacceptable he will always internally register the fact even though he may ignore it: there are circumstances and situations where a high degree of tolerance on the teacher's part will ultimately make it easier for a child to cope, but this calls for a positive policy rather than negligent lack of observation.

The use of terms like 'unacceptable' implies value judgements which in themselves can be the subject of unending discussion. Perhaps the simplest way out of this difficulty is to turn the question round and consider whether an 'unacceptable' manner in a social context might not be that which demonstrates a 'no value' judgement, where the child in his dealings either with his peers or with the teacher indicates contempt for others. The aggressive tone, the shrug of the shoulders and the dismissive stance are all common contributors to such an impression.

Of course, contempt for others is equally unacceptable when it is shown by a teacher towards the children and unfortunately children have fewer weapons for dealing with it.

WORK

Standards of work are the criteria by which schools are most commonly judged by those outside them. They are the outward and most clearly visible sign that the school is functioning well. If for no reason other than this, the wise teacher makes standards of work a matter of central concern, but his concern will be a professional one and different from that of many non-professionals in two respects. First, the standards he demands will be relative to what he knows of the children's abilities. Secondly, he will be interested in the process (the actual conduct of the activity) and not merely the product (story, graph, and so on) of the work.

Perhaps the aspect of working to be prized most highly is commitment: the performance of a task with serious intent, the concentration on the matter in hand, the perseverance to the point of completion. A child who is committed to his work will require little external supervision to keep him on the task. If these conditions are met, then the product itself is likely to bear the hallmarks of them: a piece of work showing interest, thoroughness and attention to detail.

Of course, the teacher himself bears a large responsibility to ensure that the work which children embark on allows scope for this kind of involvement. Tedious tasks lead to commonplace products. Nevertheless, it would be unrealistic to imagine that everything children do can be equally absorbing. Nor will children simply develop this commitment naturally. Rather they will require positive training and constant reinforcement throughout the year and, in the end, their attitudes to work are likely to be, in essence, a reflection of the teacher's attitudes to his own work.

TECHNIQUES

It is one thing to work out the bases for action and quite another to know how to act. There are certain principles which effective teachers can be observed to employ in the control of classes, however, which others could make use of and even elaborate. They appear to group themselves as those which relate to the conditions of learning and those which relate to the behaviour of the teacher.

CONDITIONS

The first necessary condition for a well-ordered class learning situation is that everyone in a classroom or class area has plenty to do and knows it. This is partly a matter of adequacy of provision for the work in hand and partly a matter of the profusion of additional activities available in the room. When a child finishes an allotted task, there must be plenty of other attractive things for him to do which will keep him gainfully employed. Such a system enables children both to fulfil their obligations and to show independence.

It will mean a considerable amount of preparation, forethought and planning on the part of the teacher to ensure that everything that can be predicted as needful for teacher-directed activities is to hand and that an array of self-sustaining alternative activities is also available. A great deal of time will go into the preparation of work-cards, the selection of materials and the provision of equipment. The investment pays a high return in terms of pupil involvement, however. In these circumstances, a child can work independently for indefinite periods of time. Communication and movement tend to be controlled because they are purposeful rather than simply the produce of boredom (you might as well leap about and shout if there is nothing better to do!).

A second way in which conditions conducive to learning can be created is through the use of structure in handling the class as a group. If group directions are issued without preparation, a mêlée is likely to be the result. If the group or the activity is broken down into smaller sections, much more reasonable behaviour tends to occur. Thus 'All boys with fair hair can get their milk' will produce a more ordered response than 'Everybody, get your milk'. 'Everybody stand. Now come over to the window' will probably lead to a more peaceful transfer than 'Everybody go to the window'.

Similarly, specifying a beginning or ending to an activity is helpful. 'Does everyone know what they are going to do? Off you go, then.' 'When you have got undressed for PE, sit down.'

TEACHER BEHAVIOUR

The personal qualities which the teacher can, or is prepared to, bring to the job are probably the biggest single factor in class control. Everything depends on the impression a teacher gives to the children and there are certainly two attributes which it is important for teachers to appear to possess: alertness and determination. Both convey the impression that it is just not worth going against the conventions.

Alertness is very akin to what Kounin (1970) described, in his American way, as 'withitness' which he found to be most highly related to good classroom management. Essentially, it is the ability to have eyes in the back of your head and to miss nothing unless you choose to. This is very depressing to naughty children who are then inclined to give up their naughty ways. Alertness would also include Kounin's 'overlappingness', however, which is another essential attribute especially for the teacher of young children. This is the ability to do more than one thing at once and helps maintain the flow of purposeful activity in a classroom. Most infant teachers are quite used to tying one child's shoelace at the same time as they listen to another's recital of what he did the previous evening. Junior teachers are often less used to multiple occupations.

Determination in a teacher is another quality which is depressing to naughty children for this gives the impression that he will not give up until he has made his point and that he will use all the weapons at his disposal to make it. He will wait until every child is silent before he speaks, he will reject substandard work, he will recall those who have galloped off down the corridor, he will demand a repetition of unmannerly speech, he will remind children if the noise level gets too high. All of these things he will do even though it is much less trouble not to. It is immediately much easier to give in and say 'It doesn't matter' but ultimately such a policy is costly in that the teacher is operating in a constantly unsettled situation.

The establishment of an ordered system of working and a controlled manner of behaving would be very tedious for both teacher and children if they required a constant degree of effort throughout the year. Fortunately, the major effort is required at the beginning of the year and once norms of acceptability are established, the whole process becomes much more relaxed. As time goes by, there is less and less need to be so specific about class movement. Individual transgressions can be overlooked, an understanding can develop that we all have our 'off-days'. But this kind of relaxation is the reward of early vigilance.

Almost always, as the year progresses, a teacher and a class will develop a way of relating to each other. It is the teacher's job to ensure that this involves mutual respect and understanding and is based on agreed conventions.

Mr D.

Mr D. had been teaching since completing an emergency training course after the war. In communication with adults, he was rather a gruff, awkward man and perhaps for this reason had never risen beyond the position of deputy head in a fairly small primary school. With the children, a fourth year junior class, he was strict but fair, addressing them for the most part as equals but manifesting extreme displeasure at transgressions.

His room was divided into areas, each area containing a concentration of apparatus and equipment connected with a particular part of the curriculum. So well provisioned and ordered was each area that any child could select for himself work appropriate to his level of working; thus there was never any question of idle hands. For the most part, the children worked as a class in that everyone would be doing the same subject at the same time, but as individuals in that each child, or small group of children, would be provided with a different task. If this was finished before the end of the time allotted to the subject, children would choose their own subsequent activity. These were the working conventions of the class, clearly specified and understood by all.

Equally well understood by all were the conventions governing conduct. Children worked quietly, discussing matters that arose in a mature, responsible manner. When the work required it, they moved purposefully about the school. Since they knew that they would not get away with shoddy work, it would in any case have appeared to them self-defeating to waste their time.

Mr D. and the children spoke together in the tones of people who respect each other. Of course, there were disruptions in the system from time to time since none of us is permanently reasonable. Here the displeasure of Mr D., occasionally reinforced by the denial of privileges, was sufficient to deal with the matter. Return to favour was important for all the children for they valued being part of Mr D.'s enterprise. They knew that he went to endless trouble to get them the books they needed for study, to acquire materials for new craft techniques and to gather information about matters of current interest. He would share his interests with them, taking them to gather water-weeds and insects for the fish-tank and to collect wild flowers miles away from the inner city area where they lived. He would spend hours when they were gone mounting and displaying the work that they had done. In return, they gave him respect and affection and good work.

Miss J.

Miss J. had trained about three years previously and was now in her middle twenties, a Scale 1 teacher with a vertically grouped infant class. She had a pleasant personality and related well to the rest of the staff, but it was clear from her conversation that her preoccupation with the pursuit of an active social life left little room for concern for the children she taught.

She had a large room with a sink and access to a play area outside with a sand-pit, see-saw and climbing frame. The main body of the room was taken up with tables and chairs (one chair for each child). Beyond that, there was little evidence of planning except for a library corner, a table covered with jigsaws and constructional sets and a carpeted area with an armchair in it. The walls were mostly covered with commercial pictures, material related to the reading scheme and a few unmounted children's pictures with torn edges. The general air of the room was one of untidiness since things were seldom put back in their place, even supposing anyone knew where it was, and Miss J. did not often stay long enough after school to tidy up.

The activities most frequently engaged in by the children were outside play when the weather was fine, inside play with jigsaws and constructional sets, adding-up and story-writing. While these activities were going on, Miss J. generally sat in the armchair hearing children read. Much of the rest of the time the children sat on the carpet around Miss J., singing songs or having their language developed. Whenever possible, Miss J. would ignore them, engaging in long conversations with the secretary, the caretaker and other members of staff, indeed any adult who happened to approach the room.

The children were often bored and so frequently naughty, noisy and unpleasant to each other. Miss J.'s treatment of them varied from a loud hectoring to an unlikely matyness. Since she showed so clearly that she cared very little about them, the children cared very little for her.

Chapter 3

Rewards and Punishments

Reward and punishment sound very grand terms in the primary school situation for mostly they are small things like a smile or the raising of an eyebrow. Nevertheless, their function is important, namely, to enable the teacher to control the behaviour of the children.

As teachers, we generally like to concern ourselves with intrinsic reinforcement, the rewards that children get from the actual doing of something and its successful completion. This may well be the most satisfying kind of reinforcement and we all strive to maximise it. But it would be unrealistic to suppose that in a school society it is the only kind of reinforcement at play. A school is a setting for complex behaviour and subtle personal interaction where rewarding and punishing outcomes extend far beyond the actual work situation. A teacher who wishes to remain in control must take account of the many factors which complicate the operation of reinforcement. Most successful teachers punish and reward intuitively and their methods work. A teacher who is having difficulty with control, however, may perhaps be relying on ineffective rewards and punishments or applying them inconsistently.

It may be helpful to look at the whole question of reinforcement in the light of Skinner's behaviourist theories (see, for example, Skinner, 1969). Unfortunately, the terminology tends to deter teachers, since it is so coldly clinical. Perhaps it is sufficient here to consider his basic principle that behaviour that is followed by positive reinforcement is likely to recur while that which is not is less likely to recur. By controlling the reinforcement situation, teachers can control children's behaviour.

Some would say that this is too close to manipulation to be palatable, but Skinner would claim that children's behaviour, like anyone else's, is in any case determined by the reinforcement situation and that, in this sense, we are all at the mercy of the environment. If this is so, then to exert a positive influence on the environment and, in particular, the reinforcement aspects of it (that is, rewards and punishments) is merely to recognise an existing situation and take advantage of it.

CONDITIONS OF REINFORCEMENT

Skinner established his principles largely with pigeons. Children are different from pigeons in many ways but one of the most important differences is that they have the power of speech. The pigeon cannot be told what he has to do; he must discover this by trial and error. Children can be told precisely what is expected of them, that is to say, the conditions for reward and punishment can be specified in advance.

This aspect of control cannot be emphasised too strongly. If children are feeling their way tentatively towards what might be the right thing to do, trying out all kinds of behaviour in the hope that they might hit upon the right one, then a situation of stress for both teacher and children is most likely to result. Even more stressful may be the situation where children are exploring the boundaries of unacceptability, seeing just how far they can go before retribution descends.

The stress can be avoided by a clear specification of conditions. The condition of silence, for example, is required by most teachers when they speak to the class as a whole: teacher benevolence is dependent on it. Not only does this need to be specified but the precise nature of the silence and how it will be signalled need to be demonstrated. Thus, in the early days of the school year, there is a place for what might be called 'silence practice'. The following account is an example of a teacher who is taking this precaution.

> The class has been given work to do and all have gone to their appropriate places to do it. The teacher is speaking to them. 'Now I may want to say something to you all while you are working. If I do, I shall clap my hands and then I want you to stop whatever you are doing and listen. I'll show you what I mean in a few moments. You start working and I'll stop you.'
>
> Everybody starts work and soon forgets what has been said. After a while, the teacher claps her hands and most children remember, stop their work and look towards her. Some fail to stop and carry on with what they are doing. Quickly they are reminded by other members of the class and turn towards the teacher in some confusion. She waits until she has everyone's attention. 'Well done, most of you. Not very good that table over there, or Richard and Frank. We'll try again in a few minutes' time.' Next time she claps her hands eveyone attends to her much more quickly.

This teacher has achieved two things. She has made it quite clear what her expectations are, namely, that she should receive total attention when she requires it. She has also established the way in which she will signal that this is what she wants, by clapping her hands. She has chosen this way because she does not have a very strong voice and is uncertain of her ability to make herself heard above the level of conversation that she anticipates as being normal in the classroom. As the year progresses and the children become more used to her voice, she will probably abandon the clap and merely say 'Listen, children' to collect their attention. The signal itself is not important. What is important is that there should be one.

The need to communicate expectations quite specifically applies to standards of work and conduct in all areas of school life and is particularly important in the early weeks of the school year. Along with such information must go the application of reinforcement schedules. In the example given, most members of the class are complimented (rewarded) while disappointment is expressed to a few individuals (punishment). Next time the occasion arises, those who have been rewarded are likely to repeat their successful behaviour, those who have been punished are less likely to behave in the same way.

TYPES OF REINFORCEMENT

There are basically four different classes of reinforcement: two which make it likely that behaviour will recur and two which discourage its recurrence. The presentation of something pleasurable and the removal of something unpleasant are both likely to lead to behaviour recurring. (If my dentist praises me for using dental floss, I shall be likely to use it again. If standing in front of the fire removes a feeling of cold, I shall probably look for a fire to stand in front of whenever I am cold.)

The presentation of something unpleasant and the removal of something pleasurable are both likely to discourage the recurrence of behaviour. (If I get a shock when I touch the kettle, I am unlikely to touch it a second time. If I lose my licence through careless driving, I shall probably change my driving tactics.)

Within each class of reinforcement there are many possible varieties of situation which commonly occur in the primary school. Understanding the possibilities is the first step to using them effectively.

REWARDS (1): THE PRESENTATION OF THE PLEASURABLE

The form of positive reinforcement most commonly used by all teachers is *approval*. It is a tool of tremendous variety. In its most neutral form, it consists merely in giving attention and for many young children this is a potent reinforcer. In its more positive form it ranges from the smile or the nod to the panegyric in school assembly. It is immediate in its effect, requires no preparation and is the most natural, spontaneous technique of all. It is its very spontaneity that can be its weakness, however, because for maximum effectiveness it needs to be used in a form which is appropriate not only to the behaviour but also to the child.

Fulsome praise may be encouraging to many children but to some it is offensive. We seldom overtly praise our equals; an appreciative remark or action is much more likely. There can be an element of condescension in direct praise which older or more independent and perhaps more intelligent children may resent. They may much prefer the throwaway word of commendation, or the smile of approval. They are certainly likely to prefer attention to be focused on what they have done: the discussion of a piece of work, the reading out of a story, the mounting of a picture.

It is also important for approval to be relevant to what has been done. There is a tendency particularly with younger children to hand out praise indiscriminately. Anything that is even faintly appropriate receives a 'Good boy'. In the very early stages, when the focus may be on getting the child to stay in the room at all, this may be necessary, but if it continues, as time goes by, the currency of approval is devalued. What must be required is increasingly complex and mature standards of work and behaviour and it is on improvement that approval must depend.

Personal approval can be supplemented by more tangible and impersonal rewards. These may be *object rewards*; many teachers keep a jar of sweets for special achievements and, although we do not usually think of them as such, presents for the children at Christmas are a form of generalised reward. Common, too, are *activity rewards* based on the use of an activity which the children enjoy to reinforce their performance of a task which may be less enjoyable: 'If you have finished your work, you may go and play in the bricks.' 'When everyone is sitting quietly, you will be able to go out to play.'

In some primary schools, a system of *token rewards* operates. Here the value, and hence the rewarding nature, is something which is learned and agreed upon by those concerned. Stars, badges, house points all come into this category since they have no intrinsic merit, except perhaps the pleasing shape and colour of a star, but are nevertheless accepted as tokens of approval. It is possible to extend the system further so that the tokens can be exchanged for either object rewards (Ten stars and you get a colouring book) or activity rewards (Twenty stars and you can go shopping with the teacher.)

There are those who would reject object, activity and token rewards as encouraging a selfish and materialistic attitude in children, and indeed they may be at their most appropriate in those extreme situations where other forms of reinforcement have failed. Nevertheless, used sparingly and with consideration, they can be useful tools in the armoury of the primary school teacher. Certainly, there are few of us who do not occasionally and quite naturally use object and activity rewards if only because they add variety to our ways of giving pleasure.

REWARDS (2): THE REMOVAL OF THE UNPLEASANT

This is a far less useful form of reward in the primary school as it is seldom that aversive situations are allowed to develop. Certainly they do arise at times, and then some good can be salvaged if they are treated with regard to the learning potential present. A child sitting with a dinner he does not want can be offered release if he eats a tiny agreed amount: not only is dinner-eating behaviour reinforced, but there is always the chance that he may in fact enjoy it if he tries it. A child struggling with a piece of work which he wishes he had never undertaken could be helped to conclude it in an alternative way so that completion behaviour is encouraged. In such cases the resolution of the situation follows and reinforces a positive action on the child's part rather than negative defeat.

Generally, however, this kind of reward is associated with a constructive approach to punishment. Where punishment is used to suppress an undesirable piece of behaviour, release from the punishing situation may be made attendant on the successful completion of a task: a teacher who shows displeasure (punishment) at a sub-standard piece of work may relent only when the child concerned has produced something of superior quality.

PUNISHMENTS (1): THE APPLICATION OF THE UNPLEASANT

Just as approval is the most useful and flexible form of reward in a primary school, so *disapproval* is the most useful form of punishment. Again, the variety of ways in which disapproval can be conveyed is very wide, ranging from a frown or a shake of the head to public humiliation and even physical violence. Appropriateness is even more important here for unsuitable punishment can be far more damaging than ineffective reward.

Mild disapproval of the way a child is behaving or individual criticism of a piece of work is a normal part of classroom life. Indeed, one of the most effective deterrents is merely the threat of disapproval, the quiet 'Pardon?' to the child who has spoken in an aggressive manner (he seldom repeats it without modifying his style); the anticipatory 'It doesn't look to me as if you're trying very hard with that story' to the child whose attention is clearly elsewhere.

Most children at most times need nothing more than a simple rebuke, usually more in sorrow than in anger: 'Well, I'm sorry but I don't think that will do. It's not your best, is it?' This kind of low-key disappointment is adequate for most situations.

But there are exceptional children and exceptional crimes and here the teacher who can show dramatic horror is at an advantage. The indrawn breath, the shocked expression, the ringing tones add to the effect. Where the target is a small group of children, the other children are likely to be as appalled as the teacher claims to be. Where the target is the class as a whole, if the teacher reveals his sense of shame about his class, the hardest hearts are likely to be touched.

Such histrionics are for exceptional situations, however. They depend, for their effect, on their rarity. A teacher who uses them too often creates an atmosphere of nagging and bullying.

Physical punishment is a difficult matter. Because it is so open to abuse it may be safer to rule it out altogether, but it could be argued that that may be rather like refusing to use matches in case they explode; twirling a stick in a stone is very tedious and time consuming. There may be occasions with certain children where physical punishment might be considered appropriate but this is a matter for the inexperienced teacher to discuss with the head of the school.

It is difficult to devise *activity punishments* in a primary school since such things as detention play no part in life at this level and the deliberate setting of unpleasant tasks such as writing lines seems a great waste of time. If an attempt is made to set constructive punishment tasks such as picking up litter in the playground or tidying up a cupboard, children in the primary school age range seem to enjoy these so much that they become activity rewards, thus defeating the purpose of the exercise. The setting of normal work tasks as punishments is equally dubious as it then becomes difficult to represent these as interesting and worthwhile in an ordinary class context.

Token punishments are a possibility where a school operates a points system which allows for negative as well as positive values, but it is difficult to see such a system being very effective with children other than those who respond perfectly well to a mild rebuke. The classic token punishment of the past, the dunce's cap, is fortunately no longer with us.

PUNISHMENTS (2): THE REMOVAL OF THE PLEASURABLE

There is an intermediate state between the offering of approval or disapproval which can be represented as the removal of attention, a common enough technique in the primary school. If attention from the teacher is regarded as desirable by a child, then the removal of that attention will constitute an effective punishment. Thus, much undesirable behaviour may cease if it is simply ignored. The child who tells tales will stop more quickly if the teacher takes no notice of him.

Of course, there are forms of undesirable behaviour that cannot be ignored: if one boy is kicking another, the adult present has an obligation to intervene in the interests of preserving life and limb. But these occasions are rare. There are in fact many situations where the withholding of attention would be more effective than the more positive techniques which are commonly used. The child who is refusing to take part in a PE activity, the girl who is sulking because she has not been allocated the place she wants, the boy who is crying because his teacher is away, will probably all get over the crisis if left alone and allowed to reintegrate themselves quietly with the class. Unfortunately, such behaviour often attracts to itself a good deal of teacher attention, either concern or annoyance, which may harden attitudes, making normalisation more difficult, or confirm the child in the impression that he has found an effective way of manipulating a situation.

The removal of a pleasurable activity is also a common technique with some primary school teachers. Sports and creative art and crafts activities are major candidates for removal and as an occasional measure in exceptional circumstances this may be a legitimate and useful technique. Unfortunately, the impression is conveyed that these areas of the curriculum are of secondary importance and can be missed with a clear conscience.

EXTENSIONS AND LIMITATIONS OF REINFORCEMENT

The effects of reinforcement extend beyond the immediate target in two ways. First, *vicarious reinforcement* occurs so that children considering a certain course of action will be rendered either more or less likely to undertake it when they see the reward or punishment meted out to another child. Thus, a boy will be less likely to kick a ball up on the roof when he knows that other boys have been refused permission to retrieve theirs.

Secondly, one child may *model* himself on another where the reinforcement following the other's pattern of behaviour makes it appear desirable. Thus a child may attempt to model his performance on that of his neighbour when he sees that he is praised for neat work. Equally, of course, where a child gains a position of prestige with his companions through exhibitionist behaviour, there is a likelihood that others will follow suit.

This leads us to a consideration of an important aspect of reinforcement processes, namely, their subjective nature. That which reinforces, either positively or negatively, is that which one conceives to be reinforcing. So a teacher's approval is only a reward if the child values the teacher's good opinion. It is easy to envisage a situation, particularly with older children, where the teacher is considered so alien by the children generally that praise from him acts as a form of punishment. Similarly, object and activity rewards only work if the child conceives of those objects and activities as desirable. Some children do not like lollipops and many of us would certainly regard half an hour of football as a punishment. Token systems depend entirely on their acceptance by the group and it is this which renders them so vulnerable to loss of confidence. If the group decides that they are empty rewards, stars and house points will have no value.

All of these considerations apply in reverse for punishments, of course. So the disapproval of a despised teacher or an inappropriately chosen activity can operate as rewards rather than punishments. Even physical punishment presumably acts as a reward to the masochistic child. Everything is relative to the particular child and the particular teacher.

It is an interesting exercise for any teacher to examine the way in which he uses reinforcement. In the range and variety of techniques, the way he adapts them to different situations and different children, he may surprise even himself. For the teacher who is having difficulty with control, this kind of self-examination is a necessary preliminary to any improvement. It may reveal that he must search either for more potent and durable reinforcers or for more subtle, sensitive ones; that he must improve the match between behaviour and reinforcement or increase his own acceptability as a reinforcer. This is really the heart of the matter, for where the teacher is seen by the children to be interested, concerned and hard working on their behalf, the scope for reinforcement is virtually limitless.

Chapter 4

The Physical Environment

The physical environment can have a profound effect on the way we behave. A change in the environment can bring a change in our mood or in our rate or type of activity. This provides an important opportunity for those who are in a position to arrange the environment, for by 'stage-managing' it they can hope to go some way towards managing those who live or work within it.

Those with commercial interests have been most inventive in manipulating the environment. Supermarkets tempt us to buy through skilful layout of goods; farmers play music to their cows to increase their milk yield; industrialists improve labour relations and productivity in modern factories with well-designed work benches. In schools the possible management advantages are there too but not all teachers use the environment as effectively in this respect as they might.

The kind of environment provided in the school as a whole and in a classroom or class area in particular is bound to have an effect not only on the way the people within them behave towards each other but also on the level of productive activity achieved. When all children's desks are turned to face the teacher, who is himself seated at a taller, larger desk, for instance, the implication is not only that the teacher is powerful but also that he is more important to each individual child than any of the child's peers. Relationships must at least initially be influenced by this. Where classes work in an area which is frequently required for other purposes such as eating or singing, they are likely to spend an inordinate amount of time packing up or moving out and this cannot help but affect the amount of work the children are able to get through.

These are rather obvious examples but there are a hundred and one more subtle ways in which the environment can make a statement or create conditions which affect those who work within it. Some are a product of general school factors. In this sphere there are many things which teachers and headteachers cannot control. It is difficult to do anything about winding stone staircases, high ceilings and busy roads, for example, yet all have an effect on school life. Leaking roofs, tiled walls and smelly lavatories are slightly less resistant to change although they tend to be very time consuming for the head who takes on the challenge.

Within the classroom itself the teacher who is sufficiently inventive or determined can exert a very large degree of control over the environment and hence over what goes on within it. The teacher who fails to do this not only neglects an invaluable aid in achieving his aims but may even create a handicap for himself and others working in a room: the loss of the pencil sharpener can lead to frustration and barren walls can be very depressing.

If a teacher is to take responsibility for initially creating the environment for the children who will work with him, what kind of an environment is likely to serve his purpose best? Assuming that this purpose is to ensure a harmonious community in conditions where all members can work hard with interest and commitment, he will require (1) an efficient working environment which is (2) attractive and (3) stimulating.

AN EFFICIENT WORKING ENVIRONMENT

Efficient working conditions can really only be judged in relation to the kind of work to be carried on within them. Conditions which are good for cross-country running may be quite inappropriate for the sprint. An environment planned for formal class work may contain many features which are irrelevant and even obstructive to a freer and more active regime.

Nevertheless, there are certain general principles which apply in classrooms whatever the regime in operation. These arise from the universal need to plan for a relatively large number of individuals who will be engaged in a variety of tasks during the day, who will be working at the same time and who will for the most part be answerable to and able to seek assistance from a single supervisor. The problems which are likely to arise are those concerned with such matters as allocation of space, sharing of resources, both human and material, conflict of interests and the reality of one-to-many supervision. Problems of this kind can never be completely eliminated since they are endemic in the teacher/class situation but they can be minimised through the development and exercise of independence and mutual consideration on the part of the children.

This sounds easy but how does a teacher achieve it in practice? Much of the movement towards independence and tolerance will happen as a result of the way the teacher handles children: the way he relates to them and encourages them to interact with each other. The conditions of working that he sets up, however, will also have a significant effect. The purely physical arrangement of furniture, use of space, systems of storage and retrieval can either foster or militate against the development of independence and consideration and the peacefulness of the day.

Ideally, the environment will be organised in such a way as to make the most of what is available and to avoid conflict but this needs conscious planning on the part of the teacher.

Accessibility is one of the first considerations. If the scissors are stored in a place where only the teacher can get at them, then every child will need to seek permission each time he wishes to use them. Such a situation scarcely promotes independence on the part of children.

Practicability is a second consideration. The further from water that materials for creative activities are stored, then the further water will have to be carried and the greater the likely amount of spillage. The potential for trouble and disturbance in an arrangement like this is limitless.

Social consideration is a third factor of some importance. If the room is arranged in such a way that the wood-working bench is next to the quiet library area, conditions have been created which will foster antipathy rather than harmony.

Confusions such as these seem to happen by default rather than as a result of rational planning, and in a room where due account is taken of these three principles of organisation (accessibility, practicability and social consideration) they can be reduced to the minimum. Areas of potential conflict will be eliminated and the conditions created for children to act with increasing independence.

It is one thing to accept principles of organisation as worthwhile, however, and another to apply them in practice, particularly as matters are complicated by the fact that decisions have to be made not only about *how* things are to be arranged but also about *what* things are to be arranged. At the planning stage, a theoretically empty classroom can be a daunting prospect.

A way of getting started has to be found and there is a great deal to be said for thinking about the components in terms of curriculum areas. An arrangement that can work well is for each area of subject activity to be focused on a geographical area of the room. This is helpful to the teacher in planning and conceptually easy for the children to grasp when it is put into operation. An essential prerequisite for independence is being able to understand the system: only when children know where things belong can they confidently seek them out and return them.

The subject areas may be bays created by the placing of such items as cupboards, drawer-units, storage boxes or free-standing book-shelves at right-angles to the wall or to each other. Alternatively, they may be just a table and wall space carrying pertinent material or even just a part of the room designated a specialist area by convention so that 'that is where we always have the bricks'. Of course, the activity need not be confined to this area. It is simply that the planning, execution and termination of an activity is likely to be much smoother if it is associated with a definite part of the room.

The choice of subject areas to be catered for in this way depends largely on curriculum emphases in the school or classroom. Mathematics and language, particularly written language, would be universally considered important. There might be less agreement about areas for creative activities, science, humanities, or, in the infant classroom, for forms of play. The amount of space allotted to a subject would depend both on the intrinsic demands of that subject (most forms of play demand a considerable amount of space) and on the degree of importance attached to it.

Within each area both the selection and the deployment of components can make a great difference to the ease or difficulty of life within the classroom. Clearly, the appropriateness of books, cards, equipment and materials to the tasks and activities planned is critical: it is unlikely that children will become enthusiastic voluntary readers if only dull and tattered books are available. In addition, however, it is important that what books there are should be displayed to advantage so that they appear both attractive and available. The actual deployment of the material matters. Here the secret lies partly in the choice of storage boxes, wall pockets, shelving systems, and so on, that are *appropriate* containers for whatever materials they are required to contain (bottles are no good for paints – the necks are too narrow) and that can be used *safely and confidently* by children (glass containers are always a risk). It also depends on the ingenuity of the teacher in devising ways of laying out, stacking, hanging up, leaning, suspending the materials in question and in discovering areas for display which may not be immediately apparent (all sides of a cupboard can be useful).

Finally, the furniture used as well as the way it is set out must be compatible with the regime which a teacher is trying to put into operation. Tables and chairs of the wrong size for the children may suggest lack of personalised interest. A flip chart is light, cheap and portable and may be more useful than a blackboard. One large table may make more sense than several small ones in the creative activities area. If you cannot get formica tops, perhaps vinolay might be a serviceable substitute. Does a teacher's desk justify the space it occupies? A small, lockable cupboard might fulfil the need more usefully.

A really radical reappraisal of what is required of the setting may lead to great saving of space which can be used for other purposes. It may not be necessary to have a place at a table for every child, for example, if they are not all going to be working at the same time. But there must be somewhere to collect everybody together. Could it be a carpet? And there must be somewhere for each child to keep his things. Is a multi-drawer unit the answer? These are some of the issues to be considered in the creation of an efficient working environment. Possible arrangements for an infant and a junior classroom are included as Figures 4.1 and 4.2.

A STIMULATING WORKING ENVIRONMENT

The term 'stimulating' has become a cliché in recent years but this does not invalidate the concept. Great stress has been laid throughout this section on the importance of a well-organised classroom environment but this organisation relates only to the underlying conditions necessary for getting on with the job. There is a danger, and this is that the underlying routine may assume too great an importance. The unexpected is important too because this is what provides excitement and spurs us into action. If everything is too predictable we may decline into tedious but safe responses.

So while efficient working arrangements are necessary, so are elements of novelty. Most commonly, these can be introduced within the framework of existing arrangements. It may be an intriguing object brought into the classroom (an old engine, a snake's egg). It may be a new piece of equipment (a tape recorder and headphones, a different jumping box for PE). Something usually available may be withdrawn (create a picture without paint, write a story without using your word-book).

Sometimes, however, there could be a complete suspension of normal arrangements. The environment could be transformed into something completely different: a witch's den, a space-ship, a medieval castle. Here, with everybody working on a communal project, the tasks involved both in creating the new environment and in living within it once it is created could be very different from routine requirements.

Children who are provided with the stimulus of unexpected and exciting experiences such as these will be much less likely to resort to the kind of misbehaviour that arises from boredom.

AN ATTRACTIVE WORKING ENVIRONMENT

The notion of 'attractiveness' is a very subjective one and every classroom will not be equally attractive to everyone working within it. Nevertheless, there are certain features which are appreciated by most primary school children.

Perhaps the first of these is actually having something to look at. The need to look at things of interest seems to be basic to all primates

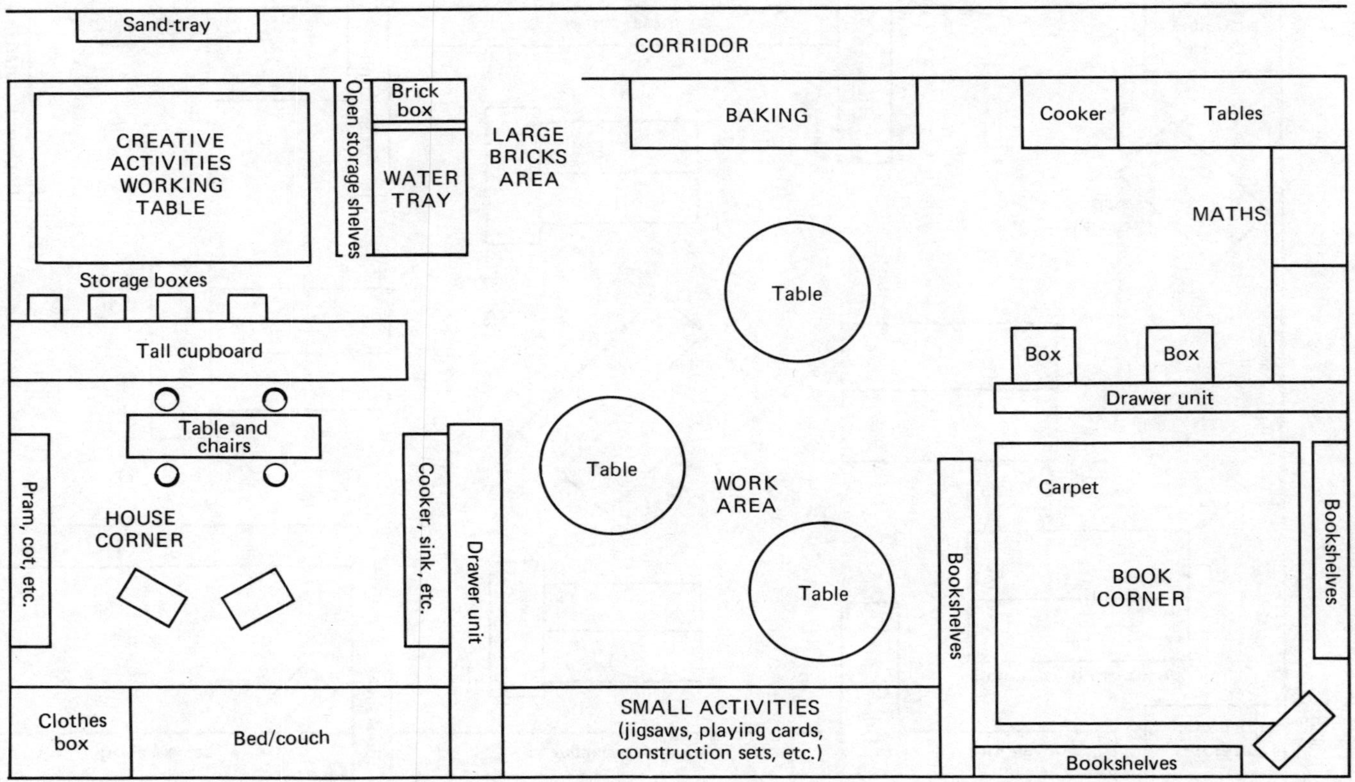

Figure 4.1 An infant classroom.

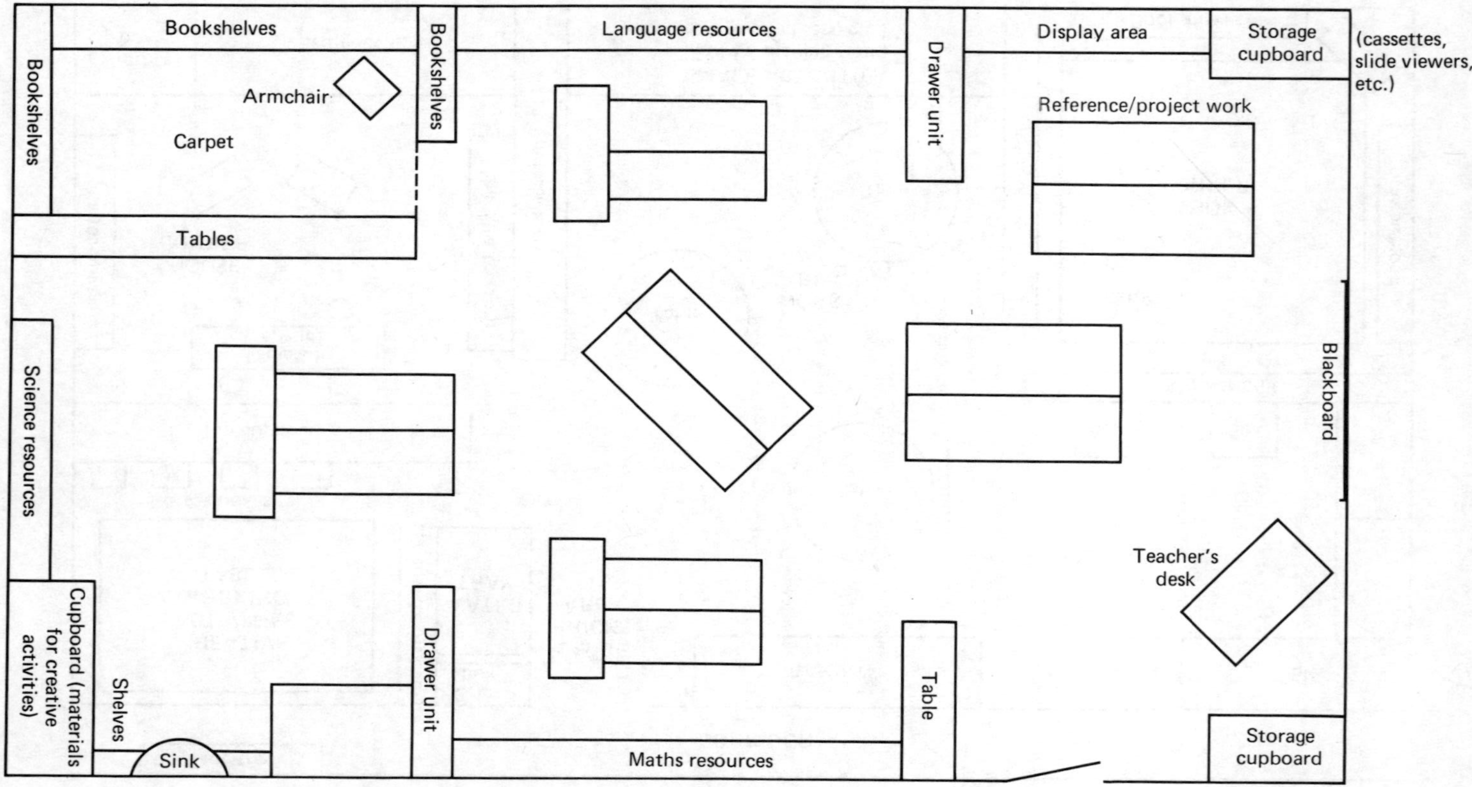

Figure 4.2 A junior classroom.

and the walls, shelves, cupboard tops, and so on, in primary classrooms offer great scope for the display of materials concerned with many different levels and areas of interest. Pictures, books, maps, charts, models, objects, specimens – the possibilities are endless and because such a variety of interests is likely to exist in a class of children and those interests may be short-lived, a rich and constantly changing display is necessary.

Colour is also a feature which seems to be attractive to most primary school children. Here commercial manufacturers have made things easy for the teacher for most materials and equipment made for use in primary classrooms nowadays provide the kind of colours which can make a room glow. The colours are there in the books and card materials, the bright plastic maths equipment, the paints and the crayons. It only remains for the teacher to bring them out in the way he arranges things and in his use of background paper and materials.

Most people are encouraged by signs that what they have done is appreciated; it is not only children who enjoy seeing their work displayed. Perhaps the most important feature in an attractive environment for a primary classroom is the children's own work, carefully mounted on the walls, set out in a position of prominence on a handy surface, suspended ingeniously from the ceiling, indeed displayed in any fashion which sets off to advantage a piece of work of which the creator may be proud.

But the onus for providing a stimulating or an attractive environment does not rest entirely with the teacher. Often, children themselves can take responsibility for a display either of their own work or of a collection of materials concerned with a current theme. Here there is a double advantage, for not only are the children helping to create the environment; they are also learning to act independently and accept the visual consequences of their actions.

Finally, the aspect of the environment that may be most attractive to children may be the evidence that their efforts are appreciated and that the teacher cares enough about them to give time to their surroundings. To find your painting on the wall tells you that your work is valued; to know that the environment you live in does not just happen but is actually created tells you that someone takes trouble over you. The teacher who really does not care about the children one way or the other can convey this very quickly by taking no interest in the environment at all. On the other hand, the teacher who wishes to strengthen his relationships with the children and to encourage good work attitudes will see this as an important factor.

Chapter 5

The Educational Environment

One of the hallmarks of a non-prospering classroom is the high level of unpurposeful activity that can be observed within it. Usually, large numbers of children are unemployed or at the least underemployed. Some may be working sluggishly, depressed by sheer boredom; some may have finished or reached an impasse in an allotted task and may be waiting for the teacher's attention; some may be taking advantage of the teacher's harassment (for in such a classroom teachers are usually bowed down by the demands made upon them) and may simply have abandoned their work for more exciting pursuits. There may be a general feeling that it does not matter very much as the work is seldom checked: the teacher just does not have time. Even those who try to work may well find themselves impeded by the fact that they have to wait for a piece of equipment that someone else is using or that there are too many people trying to carry out a task in an area which is too small to hold them. The overwhelming impression is that something has gone wrong with the ebb and flow of activity and that whatever kind of regulatory system exists it is not operating successfully.

An effective system depends on a shared understanding between the two parties in the situation, the children and the teacher. Each must agree to certain standards of work and behaviour and certain levels of personal constraint and co-operation, and underlying all these they must share a fundamental expectation of success.

Children who expect to be successful work confidently. They are likely to be those who are constantly encouraged and whose past experience under the guidance of the teacher has led them to expect success. They know that they will not get away with sub-standard work but will always be expected to produce something in keeping with their level of ability. In the course of working, they will be expected to devote themselves seriously to the task in hand and to finish what they have started. There is an acceptance that however free the regime might appear to be, there are certain work requirements to be fulfilled and there are well-defined limitations on their choice of activity. In the course of their work they may be obliged at one time to share resources with others and at another to respect the rights of others to sole use of a resource. They will willingly help someone who needs help which they are able to give.

Once conventions such as these are established, the whole enterprise can go on to automatic pilot whenever it suits the teacher. Everything will move purposefully along. The question is, how do such conventions come to be established? Again, much of the secret lies in the way the teacher interacts with the children, but the working situation in which such interaction happens is also important.

The kind of work devised, when and for how long it occurs, how it is allocated, the way children are grouped and the way the teacher uses his time: all these factors are important in establishing a system of working which will foster confidence, independence and commitment on the part of children. It is difficult for a child even to know whether he has been successful if the teacher is never on hand to check and comment on his work. It is difficult for him not to become bored or naughty if he is constantly waiting for someone to finish with something he requires, if he needs help and has nowhere to get it and if he easily runs out of things to do.

What is needed is a system which is based on as much foresight as possible so that the likely demands of the work in hand are anticipated and arrangements are made which will cater adequately for those demands. The whole operation is to a large degree one of matching among the three important factors in the situation: the child, the teacher and the task.

CHILDREN - TASK

The primary level of matching must, of course, be between the child and the task. What the child is required to do must be suitable for his stage of development and his previous experience in so far as the teacher can know these. There is little point in giving an infant reading material which explores the problems of adolescence or encouraging a junior to do large-piece wooden jigsaw puzzles. Unless these are highly exceptional children, such experiences are unlikely to provide scope for growth, however convenient they may be at the time.

In addition to a match between a child and an individual task, there is also a need for a match between children and overall schedules. There is some danger that if the scrutiny is only of individual tasks, a child could end up with a sequence of tasks which all demanded a similar response such as writing or all involved him for a similar length of time. This kind of sequence is unlikely to appeal to the taste which most primary school children have for variety. A child's total programme for the day should bring him a balanced and varied selection of tasks which take account of both his tastes and his best interests.

A further important question is that of what children will actually be required to do in the performance of a given task and how this will relate to what others are doing at the same time. Will there be any conflict in the activities, use of space and use of materials envisaged? One group involved in musical composition may be very disturbing to another which is trying to solve a mathematical problem; the same floor space cannot be occupied by painters and measurers; the same scales cannot be used by children doing mathematics and those baking cakes. Are there enough of the materials required? It is no good planning timing work for six if there are only five clocks; a working group cannot complete their weighing if those in the Wendy house have got all the dog biscuits. These kinds of problems can be easily avoided so long as a thorough examination of work planned has revealed their possible existence.

TEACHER – TASK

What demands will any given activity make on the teacher? How much of his attention will be required and at what point in the proceedings? An experienced teacher develops the capacity to deal with many things at the same time but he needs to be able to focus his attention on a chosen individual or group of children when he considers it necessary. This freedom is only possible if activities in the rest of the room are arranged in such a way as to make the other children substantially independent of him.

Getting the balance of attention right can make all the difference between a successful day and an exhausting, unproductive one. Pairing practical maths for some children with mechanical maths for others, hearing the really slow readers when others are engaged in writing: these are the ways that a teacher can plan to distribute his attention during the day. Nothing need suffer: those children or those activities which do not get the attention today may get it tomorrow.

CHILDREN – TEACHER

In terms of establishing a working system, the important matter to decide between teacher and children is who actually determines what the children will do. How far is it reasonable for the teacher to dictate what children should do and when they should do it in a situation where we are claiming to encourage initiative and independence?

A school class is a community for which the teacher bears a responsibility and a balance needs to be struck between the demands of the individual (teacher or child) and those of the community. There must inevitably be constraints. No single person, adult or child, can do precisely what he wants to do every moment of the day. One child cannot be allowed to play a cassette recorder next to another who wants to read; twenty-five children cannot all show their work to the teacher at the same time; an infant cannot be allowed to play with the bricks all day and every day. So there are bound to be many infringements of personal liberty with the teacher acting as lawgiver and arbitrator in both the short and long term interests of the children.

But what about the actual work they do? Should children have a large say in the work that they do or does it remain the professional responsibility of the teacher, in the light of his knowledge and experience as an adult, to decide this?

There is no easy answer. It may be that we work best at things to which we are committed but need these be things that we have actually chosen or devised ourselves? Most teachers see it as their responsibility to plan the major work load of the class, even if they are pleased to deviate from this in the face of unanticipated enthusiasms. But children's choice is important and indeed can be built in as a major organisational factor.

One way is to provide for two levels of activity in the classroom: that which fulfils the teacher's demands and that which consists of self-chosen activities. When the first level has been completed, children can progress to the second level which can include a whole range of activities, for example, reading, maths, or language cards, constructional sets, painting, use of audio-visual equipment. The materials for optional activities should be attractive and not too taxing in nature, their main function being to provide a system of consolidation and scope for independent functioning, although the occasional use of such supplementary material as main-task material may help to increase its prestige, particularly in the eyes of young children. The only requirements for optional activities need be that children can set them up themselves and that they need no checking, are self-checking, checked by another child, or need only to be swiftly scanned by the teacher. If this is the case, then they provide a support system which ensures that children are never unemployed, yet does not place extra demands on the teacher at the beginning or end of a busy session.

From the matching exercise suggested above certain recurring themes emerge:

(1) Activities planned for children should relate to them as individuals with particular strengths and weaknesses, experiences and interests.

(2) If due account is taken of the nature and requirements of activities, many areas of potential conflict can be avoided.

(3) A teacher's attention can be deployed as can any other resource if an attempt is made to predict the likely demand on it.
(4) While the teacher must retain overall responsibility for work, child-selected activities can aid the smooth operation of the system.

A working system in a primary school classroom could profitably incorporate all these principles but the synthesising of them is often difficult, and here it may help to give attention to other planning dimensions such as timing and grouping which can help to co-ordinate the whole system.

TIMING

Timing concerns both the day as a whole and the detail of each individual working session. It may be helpful to think of the day as consisting of three major parts:

(1) early morning (9 a.m. until playtime)
(2) late morning (playtime until dinner-time)
(3) early afternoon (dinner-time until playtime).

The final portion of the afternoon (playtime until home-time) is generally quite brief and in most schools is taken up with a relaxing activity such as story-time or discussion.

In most schools, two of the three major working periods of the day are given over to routine work while the third tends to be taken up with a non-routine activity.

NON-ROUTINE PERIODS

This may be an unexpected happening such as a visit from the nurse or a particularly long school assembly. More usually, however, it will be devoted to one of the multitude of activities which compete for time and space on the primary school timetable. Physical education, music and drama and creative activities are the main contenders for this period of time. The label *non-routine* by no means implies *non-essential* but simply that the organisation and arrangements required for these activities will be rather different from those required for the rest of the day.

There will be many times when this non-routine period is not enough to cater for all that a teacher wants to get into it in which case he will need to push some of the activities into other periods of the day. A short PE session, for example, could occur in the middle of one of the routine periods, but this can happen without major interruption: children become quite used to leaving everything and then picking up where they left off on their return. Similarly, creative activities can occur in the routine part of the day but it is unlikely that this would eliminate the need for separate sessions. The teacher's attention at such times will most probably be elsewhere and it is as important to introduce children to new ideas and techniques in creative activities as it is in any other area of the curriculum.

Conversely, many non-routine activities do not quite fill the time available. PE or singing, for example, would seldom occupy an hour, even allowing for preparation and change of location. This leaves a small parcel of time which is very valuable. Indeed, on the days when it does not occur naturally, it may be necessary to create such a time. These are the times when the class can be together discussing something of common interest, listening to each other, learning how to perform a new mathematical activity (using a spring balance, for example), carrying out one of the many reading activities which are fun to do as a group (scanning a passage for answers, building up phonic skills, and so on). At such times, too, a teacher can spend a few minutes with a group while everyone else reads purely for pleasure. A bright child will often be pleased either to listen to, or read to, a slower child.

These could be the times when a child may carry on with a project which he has undertaken. He may be investigating a topic by means of reference books; he may have started work on a 'novel'. Such schemes often absorb every spare moment a child can find.

ROUTINE PERIODS

The remaining two periods of the day can be given over, in the main, to a working routine. Here the children will be engaged both in the tasks which the teacher has allocated and in those which they have chosen for themselves. The degree of variety in the tasks and the length of time children spend on a single task will depend very much on the age and intellectual calibre of the children and the importance the teacher attaches to the skill or knowledge involved.

It is in the two working sessions of the day that the detail of timing becomes important. Most particularly, the starting and finishing of these sessions can be very taxing.

Starting

Some sessions start with everybody together, listening, watching, or taking part in discussion. There is no problem here. Neither is there a problem if everyone then proceeds to respond in a similar way: to write a report, to draw a picture. The problem begins when the responses are going to be different in kind or where the children are, from the start, involved in very different activities. Here, as well as ensuring that necessary resources are available and that activities do not conflict, it is important to achieve a smooth flow of traffic to the various activities. This can be helped by making sure that each child knows what he is going to do before the class group breaks up and can provide himself with whatever he needs to do it.

But the preliminary allocation process can become very tedious if it is too lengthy. One way of cutting it to the minimum is by using every possible aid to supplement the teacher's instructions and influence. Directions, stimuli, conditions and information can all be written or taped so that they are available as elaboration of the teacher's briefing or for consultation during the course of the session. This also helps in the maintenance of a smooth flow once the session is under way.

The process is also helped by thorough preparation on the part of the teacher so that not only does he have a plan for the day, but also he has made sure that every requirement that can be anticipated has been catered for. The cards, books, apparatus, equipment, and so on, that can be predicted as necessary for each session are there before the session begins, either to hand for the teacher or in a known and accessible place where they can be found by the children themselves.

Finishing

Finishing a period of work can present even more problems than beginning it. There are many reasons for this. First, putting away complex or extensive equipment is usually more demanding than getting it out. Secondly, individuals do not all conveniently complete a piece of work at the same time. Thirdly, there will be a great deal of checking and inspection to be carried out. (Every morsel of attention given to work at the time it is done and in the presence of the worker can be worth whole evenings of solitary marking.) How can so many competing demands be satisfied?

Realistically, of course, they never can be completely, but some ways of organising enable a teacher to cope with them better than others.

Clearing away is partly a matter of training and partly of convention. Training can be carried out in the non-routine sessions when an abundance of materials may be in use but where the teacher can plan to concentrate wholly on the process of clearing up in the final minutes. What is learned there can be expected to transfer to the routine sessions where less attention is available. With younger children it may even pay to have specifically set-up training sessions where the object of the exercise is for the children to learn the routine of clearing away.

The kind of conventions that prove useful are, first, that there is a known place to which everything must be returned and a known state in which things are to be left, whether it be a painting table or a set of Cuisenaire rods; second, that things are put away as they are finished with rather than left to the end, so that they do not become overwhelming in quantity; and third, that for most routine sessions, there is an embargo on those items such as modroc plaster or meccano sets which require more than average supervision either in use or in clearing away. It is, in any case, a good idea to keep some 'treats' for the non-routine sessions.

The problem of checking work is twofold: what to do with those who have not finished and how to see everybody's work. This is where problems of control arise particularly frequently as children wait for attention or decline into a state of depression as they struggle on to complete their work. There is no easy solution but the following ideas might be worth consideration:

(1) If a teacher gives close scrutiny to as much work as possible while it is in the process of being carried out, he will already have a good idea of the standard achieved and the child will have a good idea of his assessment of it. Final inspection will be merely a formality.

(2) In a routine working session, arrangements can be made to ensure that a whole classful of finishing-times do not occur at the same time. Not everybody needs to begin at the same time; account can be taken of the demands of the work to be done and the varying abilities of the children so that finishing-times are staggered. Moreover, not everybody needs to be involved in the kind of activity that needs formal checking anyway. Some might be painting, working with constructional equipment, or tape-recording a story while others are writing.

(3) This kind of flexibility is greatly aided by the strategic use of the self-selected activities mentioned previously. They can be used, as suggested above, to fill in the spaces around teacher-directed activities. They can involve children before they begin their main task or after it is completed. Because of the requirement of minimum checking, they will not complicate the process of finishing but will simply contribute positively to the smooth flow of the session and make the staggering of work completion more attainable.

(4) The teacher's planning for stress-free finishing-times will all be in vain unless the children co-operate. Those who do not finish their work within the allotted time can make things very difficult. It is certain that there is an immense variation in the speed with which any individual may decide to work and a warning, perhaps five or ten minutes before finishing-time, often encourages

children to pace themselves in such a way as to finish on time.

(5) There will still be those who have not finished and here a decision has to be made about why they have not finished. It may be because of a continuing involvement in their work, in which case there seems to be no reason why they should not carry on either during the following session or whenever it is next convenient. It may be because the task has proved too difficult, in which case, if an honourable effort has been made, some way of winding up the activity can be found: 'just finish the one you're on', 'that will do for today', and so on. It may be, on the other hand, that the child has largely wasted his time, in which case he may be allowed to put the work to one side for the moment but required to continue it during the course of an activity which he normally regards as desirable.

(6) Often the pressure associated with trying to finish a routine session comes from the awareness that playtime or dinner-time are on hand. At dinner-time the pressure is usually made inevitable by meal arrangements but at playtime it is likely to come from the need for a break. Yet the whole situation may be to some extent circular for the need for a break is increased by the pressure to finish the session. In some schools, the pressure is eased by having a drink brought round to staff. The very fact that most children have gone out into the playground is a break in itself and usually there is still time for communication with other adults in the corridor or in a nearby classroom when the stragglers have been dealt with. Such a system can be less stressful than dashing off to a staff-room.

(7) Finally, when the type of work involved is not conducive to any of these measures, it is useful to have an agreed point of deposit for work that needs to be looked at so that everyone has a routine to follow in the closing moments of a session.

GROUPING

It is not always necessary for children to work in groups. Sometimes it is more appropriate for them to work as a class, each individual responding at his own level. Such an arrangement is certainly likely to reduce to the minimum difficulties of control.

For many activities, however, it will be necessary, if all children are to derive maximum benefit from them, for the class to be divided into groups. This may be so that work at a suitable level for children of similar ability can be devised or it may be that an activity such as group discussion is planned, involving interaction and co-operation amongst the children taking part. In either case, the class as a whole will need to be broken down into smaller units.

Here it may be helpful to draw a distinction between group organisation at the planning stage and group organisation at the operational stage. Distinctions which are clear in the planning mind of the teacher need not be evident when plans are put into operation. Constantly changing working combinations and care never to refer to groups in such a way as to suggest ability ratings will help to obscure children's awareness of distinctions. Of course, it is never possible to shield children completely from a knowledge of where they stand in relation to others and nor would we wish to do so. Independence may be an aim but it needs to be realistic independence. Nevertheless, it is possible to preserve open horizons and a sense of worth in children by ensuring that nobody is consigned to a lifetime of working with 'Group F'.

The number of groups a teacher uses for planning will vary according to the size and ability range of the class. At the beginning, it may be best to limit the number of groups to three to cater for the majority of the class plus a collection of individuals at the top and another at the bottom end of the class. The basis for the allocation to groups will depend largely on the information available but reading ability is a useful, rule-of-thumb guide. If a poor reader has great facility with numbers he can be allocated work with a higher group in mathematics, but cases such as this are unusual.

Having established the groups, the teacher can then plan learning experiences for them, scrutinise the likely demands that each group will make on his attention and plan the day or week accordingly.

Sometimes, it may be best to have all children working on the same activity if there is a natural distribution of demand during the course of the session. Story-writing, for example, might work out like this. After the initial stimulus, an able child would get on with his writing, requiring the teacher's help with words from time to time but in the main being self-sufficient until the end when he would expect the teacher to read his story. A child of average ability would also get on alone at first but would probably exhaust himself quite soon and would then require a lot of attention in the sorting out of his story. A slow child might still be at the stage where it is necessary for the teacher to give a great deal of help at the beginning, even writing his dictated story so that he can copy underneath. The demand for attention would thus be distributed evenly over the beginning, middle and final phases of the session.

Sometimes, it pays to combine deliberately activities which will demand differing levels of teacher attention. Reference work for the brightest children may require a moderate but constantly recurring involvement from the teacher. This could be combined with activity for other groups which make similarly moderate demands: practical mathematics for the middle group; reading work-books or work-sheets for the poorest. An activity which demands intensive involvement from the teacher, for example, phonic work with a middle ability group, could be combined with activities for the others which demand little teacher attention: mechanical mathematics for the most able and illustration for the slowest, for example.

It was suggested earlier that children do not always need to work in the same groups even though the teacher plans for them as groups. If a teacher wants to give a great deal of individual attention to a few children with a particular learning problem, these could be extracted from their normal group. The remaining members of the group could then work with a different group on an activity such as a reading laboratory which caters for a wide span of ability.

It may in any case be desirable to set up heterogeneous groups if the strength of the planned activity lies in interaction of group members. Discussion to aid reading comprehension, for example, may benefit from a wide ability range. In such a situation, the teacher would probably want to be present for most of the time, in which case he might allow all the other children to work on self-selected activities.

Once a teacher begins to plan in a flexible way to allow himself to take full advantage of the differing demands made at different times by children of differing abilities, he is likely to find that his capacity for strategically juggling the children will grow as the year progresses. It is an area where description is more complex than actuality and practice simplifies the whole process.

THE EXTRAORDINARY DAY

The aim so far has been to examine factors which play an important part in the establishment of a routine which enables both teacher and children to give of their best. The danger is that the routine may become so tightly and efficiently organised that it acquires a life of its own and variety is regarded as disruption; children have, and know, their place in the system and are as reconciled to their circumscribed repertoire of behaviour as battery hens. 'When the pink cards are finished, you go on to the blue; when you've done writing, you do maths.'

To guard against this kind of stultifying rigidity and to ensure variety, a teacher needs to be on the lookout for ways to adapt the routine and for opportunities to abandon it altogether.

Sometimes it pays to capitalise on adverse circumstances. If the class is decimated by measles and only fifteen turn up, this may be a good time to spend half a day checking through small apparatus (construction sets, cards, and so on), the library, or the weighing materials. Such activities offer great scope for purposeful sorting and classifying operations. If one of the children is feeling antisocial, it might be a good idea to do an extended physical education session: by the time he has been working strenuously for half an hour or so, he probably will have little energy left for hostility.

Not all unplanned situations are adverse, however, and it is just as possible to capitalise on good luck. The sun is shining and it feels like the first day of spring: why not drop everything and spend the afternoon in the park or on the croft? A local factory is getting rid of a lot of polystyrene so why should not everyone make a picture, a print, or a model from it? One of the girls has a new record for her birthday: a record session may lead to very exciting dancing, writing, or painting.

A skilful teacher understands the value of opportunism and will draw sound learning experiences from the most unlikely happenings, but he will probably also actively plan for the unusual occasion. If a story has gripped the imagination of the class as a whole, everyone may enjoy contributing to a large composite picture; a morning at the station is a natural accompaniment to any study of travel; the exploration of a newly introduced theme can totally involve everybody for the whole of the day. The key to operating these planned 'extraordinary days' lies, as with routine days, in thoughtful organisation.

Not all extraordinary days would demand a total abandonment of the system, however. Sometimes it may be only the teacher who is aware of the day as extraordinary as he allocates his time in an unusual way: teachers as well as children enjoy changes in routine. It may be that he decides to cut supervision of work groups to the minimum and be available to children in the play areas of an infant room. This will not only have the effect of imparting adult stimulus and adult language into the play situation; it will also enable the teacher to survey and assess, in detail, what is happening in the various play areas, gathering information which will help in planning any reorganisation or introduction of materials.

Another day he may decide to allocate work of a fairly mechanical self-checking type to all children, knowing that while the novelty of the situation will ensure involvement on the part of the children, he will be free to devote himself to another activity such as hearing every child read. This will again provide an opportunity for looking at the overall situation which may aid him logistically in his approach to reading.

Children often find it fun to have a 'pretend the teacher isn't here' session. They are left to organise themselves completely while the teacher affects to be busily occupied with something else. It is revealing at such times to see which children give up first and find it impossible to continue without teacher attention.

The possibilities for modifying or abandoning the routine are endless and rewarding to explore for the importance of novelty and variety for both children and teacher should never be overlooked.

Many of the secrets of successful child management lie in the nature of the learning activities planned and the way they are combined. Where activities are unsuited to the individual child, where they conflict in their demands on resources and personnel and with each other, problems are bound to arise. On the other hand, productive and comparatively stress-free days can be brought about by thoughtful consideration of the individual and his needs and imaginative anticipation of what is involved in carrying out the activities planned.

A MORNING IN AN INFANT CLASS

A whistle blows in the yard but there is little noticeable effect in the top infant classroom. Most of the children are already inside. Some have their mothers with them and are reading to them or showing them a piece of work in their book or talking to them about a picture on the wall. Others are reading in the library corner, doing jigsaw puzzles, or just chatting together.

The teacher finishes listening to a boy reading and goes over to an armchair in the library corner. Most of the children sit down on the carpet around her and as the mothers leave she calls the stragglers over to her. The register is dealt with quickly and the teacher introduces the 'sound for the day'. *OU* is written on the large flip chart next to the teacher and discussion and examples follow. Some examples are written down but plenty of space remains for the children to add to these at various times during the day. A 'special' pen – the teacher's own felt-tipped pen – is left beside the chart for this purpose.

After a few minutes the teacher realises that it is time for school assembly and tells the tallest children to line up at the door. When they have established a quiet, orderly row, she sends the others to line up beside them. The children move off down the corridor to the hall, chatting quietly to each other. The teacher is with the children at the front so that she can establish a seemly procession to the hall.

When assembly is over, the children sit down again on the carpet and the teacher tells half the children to get their work-books and sit at the work-tables. These are two of the brightest children, two of the slowest, and the large middle group. As they sort themselves out the rest of the children are asked to name their choice of activity, conflicts are resolved and they depart. Most of them opt for play areas such as the large bricks, the sand- or water-trays, or the house corner but some choose to read or to work from cards. For the rest of the session, they will select their own activities within the limitations established by the teacher. They can change to alternative activities if places are available or an exchange can be agreed. If they leave an area empty they are responsible for tidying up before they go.

The teacher joins the group at the work-tables and gives to the slow children a set of matching cards aimed at increasing their sight vocabulary. They have used this type of card material before and are able to get straight on with the work. To the two brightest children she returns the rudimentary reference work they began the day before, with suggestions for how they can develop it. She then devotes the next ten minutes to mathematics teaching with the middle group. From time to time she needs to attend to an incident in the self-selecting group, and once she glances at the matching activity to check that it is being accurately completed, but in the main, she is undisturbed.

When she has finished with the middle group, they proceed to work on the topic she has introduced. This involves weighing various parcels and recording and working on the results. She is now free to devote a little time to the matching activity, hearing the children read the words and commenting on their writing and drawing performance as they record their results. After this, she spends some time discussing progress and direction with the two children doing reference work.

Anticipating that she will shortly have a little time to listen to children reading, she calls two children from the self-selecting group to get their reading-books and prepare a page. As they do this, she returns to the middle group to satisfy herself that all is going well. By now, the two matching children have finished. Their work needs only a brief check as the teacher has already been through it with them and they put it away and pass into the self-selecting group. In return, two more of the less able children are called to begin work on a similar matching task.

Now there is a brief lull during which the teacher can listen to the children who are ready with their reading books and call two more to prepare. As they do this, she encourages members of the middle group to complete their maths work and show it to her. Again, she already has an idea of how they are doing from her previous inspection but as the work here is new, she is likely to have more to discuss with each child than she did with the matching children. As she finishes with each child, she sends him to get on with some phonic work-sheets which he began the day before.

When the changeover is complete, she listens to the two children who now have pages ready. (Had the changeover taken longer than anticipated, she would have sent them back into the self-selecting group until she was ready.) She then returns to the second round of matching children and goes through their work with them before leaving them to complete their recording.

Time is running out and she announces to the class as a whole that it

PLANNING FOR THE INFANT MORNING – ROUTINE SESSIONS

High achievers (4) (2) Reference work L ------ I -------- H ------------ (2) self-selecting		PLAYTIME	self-selecting Reference work L -------- I ------------------ H	
Upper group (6) self-selecting			Instructions for jam; mechanical maths H -------- I -------- L ---------	
Middle group (10) Weighing activity; phonic sheet H -------- I -------- L----------			self-selecting	
Lower group (6) self-selecting			Reading work-sheets; measuring L -------- H -------- I ---------	
Low achievers (2) Matching I ------ (2) self-selecting	(4) self-selecting Matching I --------------		(4) self-selecting	Plastic blocks H ---- I ----

Notes (*a*) L, I and H refer to Low, Intermittent and High in terms of degree of teacher attention required.
When groups are on self-selecting (play) activities minimal teacher attention is assumed.

(*b*) Numbers in brackets refer to numbers of children in groups.

(*c*) The whole of the high achievers' working time is given over to reference work on this particular morning. This can be counterbalanced by a whole session spent on maths another day.

will be time for milk in a few minutes. She has a few moments then to listen to one or two of the better readers who do not need time to prepare pages and then proceeds to encourage everyone to pack up.

The self-selecting group do so with very little fuss, get their milk and drink it. In the work group, the teacher can deal with the matching and phonic sheet children at a glance and devote some time to discussion with the children doing reference work. Gradually, the children finish their work and leave for the playground. Finally, the last two children put their work away and the teacher wanders out to talk with her infant school colleagues in the corridor.

After playtime, a similarly organised routine session takes place where those who were at the work-tables previously now become the self-selecting group. The upper and lower groups work now and two more of the particularly able children carry on with the beginnings of reference work. The teacher spends a little time in discussion with these two children, will return to them briefly during the session and then again at the end. The upper group begins with writing instructions for making cherry jam, an activity carried out the previous day. This requires a lot of discussion which involves the teacher. When the writing is finished, they pass on to practice in mathematical computation. The lower group begin with work-sheets which relate to their current reading-books and carry on to complete some measuring activities which they began the day before. Halfway through the session, the four slower children are called from the self-selecting group and, after some preparation with the teacher, begin work on tasks related to plastic number blocks.

As the session draws to a close, the teacher has briefly to check the mechanical work of the upper group and the number work of the four slowest children. She will have been working with the measuring group so will not need to assess their work. This will leave her free to spend the closing minutes with the two children doing reference work.

A MORNING IN A JUNIOR CLASS

When the whistle blows, many of the boys are still in the yard playing football but a few are already in the classroom and many of the girls are inside. Some of the class are about the school performing tasks for which they are responsible but they return to their own room.

As they come into the classroom, they join those already there in tackling a brief series of graded mental arithmetic problems which await them on a duplicated sheet. The register is completed, the teacher listens to one or two of the children reading and then quickly goes through the arithmetic sheet. By this time, other classes can be heard on their way to assembly. The teacher stands by the door and calls them to come over to him with a partner. Most children have their favourite partner and the process is quick and easy.

After assembly the class return to their places and the teacher indicates that the most able group (together with the small collection of particularly able individuals, who do not really fit in any group) should choose their own activity to begin with. Most of them decide to read although one or two continue with the arithmetic sheet which they began before assembly, and two boys carry on with the report of Saturday's football match which they are writing up from their notes for the class newspaper.

The teacher gives a packet of mechanical maths cards to the middle group knowing that these will act for them as consolidation of newly acquired skills. They settle down quickly to this.

He gives a small bag of coins (which he is sufficiently realistic not to leave permanently available on the maths table) and some cards setting tasks concerned with composition of money to the group of individuals who are experiencing difficulty with maths. They begin immediately to sort out the money and to work out what the cards require them to do: the instructions are largely visual so by conferring they are able to make some sense of them.

Meanwhile, the lower group is examining the clocks and clock stamps which have been placed on their working table. The teacher arrives and spends the next ten minutes or so going over the recording of time which he discussed with the class as a whole a few days previously but which he suspects this group has not completely grasped. He leaves them with work to do and passes on to the money group. Here he finds that the children are making reasonable progress but are stuck on a question concerned with giving change from 20 pence. He sorts this out, has a word of encouragement with the middle mechanical maths group and then calls for all those involved in self-selected activities. They put away what they are doing and come over to him.

He has devised for them a series of tasks requiring information about a group of objects to be inferred from a single object. (Given a penny, how many pennies in a metre? Given a marble, how many marbles in a kilo?) He discusses this type of problem with them and they work through an example together, recording the stages as they go. He leaves them with a collection of objects and cards bearing questions relating to them and the group set out together in pairs to tackle the problems. When they need weighing or measuring equipment they get it, and for the rest of the session, apart from occasional consultations with the teacher, they remain largely self-sufficient.

The teacher goes to the middle group where the children are checking their own answers as they complete the cards. He spot-checks the card each child is on and goes over any difficulty he encounters. Most children are advised to complete their current card and then choose something of their own to do: almost everyone

PLANNING FOR THE JUNIOR MORNING – ROUTINE SESSIONS

Group	Activities				
High achievers (3) self-selecting	Problem tasks H ---- L -------------------------------- H	PLAYTIME	Operate as class	Operate as individuals
Upper group (8) self-selecting	Problem tasks H ---- L -------------------------------- H			
Middle group (8) Mechanical maths L ---- I --------------------- H	self-selecting			
Lower group (6) Time work H ---- L ----------------------------------- H	self-selecting			
Low achievers (4) Money work L ---- H ---- I -- H	self-selecting			

Notes (*a*) L, I and H refer to Low, Intermittent and High in terms of degree of teacher attention required. When groups are on self-selecting activities minimal teacher attention is assumed.

(*b*) Numbers in brackets refer to numbers of children in groups.

chooses to remain with the spirit of the session and some choose number puzzles which the teacher has compiled and left in a special box and some choose to measure parts of their body. The teacher feels that one or two children have not worked on the set cards as well as they might have done, however, and they are required to continue with the task.

Gradually, the teacher works his way through the time and money groups, checking each child's work. Generally the child is then allowed to transfer to self-selected activities, but occasionally he is required to persist.

When it is nearly milk-time, the most able group are advised to finish the task they are doing and the teacher looks over their efforts before they put them away; they will complete this work the following day. Those on self-selected activities begin packing up and drinking their milk and finally the teacher reaches agreement with the stragglers still working from the different groups. He is on playground duty and therefore ushers everybody out in good time.

After playtime, the teacher begins a discussion about furry animals, building up ideas, vocabulary and anecdotes, preparatory to setting the children off on writing stories. The idea catches fire and most of the class begin to write enthusiastically. One or two of the less able children need help in sorting out their ideas and getting together the words to express them. The teacher sees to them and then there is a period of relative peace while children write, using word-books, lists and banks to find the words which present difficulties and only approach the teacher as a last resort. This allows him to listen to several of the children reading.

As children begin to finish, he goes over their stories with them, discussing difficulties and suggesting improvements. Some of them begin to transcribe an improved copy into their story-books; others are waiting to consult with the teacher and as they wait they read; yet others continue to write. At the end of the morning, all children bring their papers or books to the teacher so that he can go over those he has not already seen and talk to the children about them at the earliest opportunity. Those he has seen are left at the agreed collecting-point beside him.

Chapter 6

The Peer Group

Earlier, it was suggested that the physical environment within which people function can have a profound effect on the way they behave. Equally, it can be argued that the human environment significantly affects an individual's performance. The human environment for the individual pupil in a classroom consists principally of the teacher and other children. Both of these elements are likely to influence the pupil but each to differing degrees at different ages and in different regimes. The influence is also likely to depend on the way the teacher and the peer group interact with each other. A teacher and peer group who are united in outlook may be more influential than either party separately.

The peer group for a child can vary in size according to the situation. It may consist of the total class group or of the working group which constitutes his immediate personal environment. Of course, this allows for possible conflict between the two levels of peer group: if the class as a whole wishes to go out to play but John's group votes to carry on painting, he may be in something of a dilemma until he decides which of the two groups he will conform to. Either way, he may feel alienated from one group or the other.

The strength of the peer group is likely to change with age. When the child first enters school his outlook will almost inevitably be, in Piagetian terms, egocentric, that is to say, he will see the world predominantly from his own perspective. Things will appear to revolve round him and the other children in his class will be less important in terms of influence than they will later become. His teacher will be a figure of considerable importance whom he will assume to be preoccupied with his (the child's) concerns. He will tend to see things in terms of black and white; ways of behaving will be wholly good or wholly bad and he will take the lead for these judgements from his teacher. If she is scandalised by an act of naughtiness, he will tend to accept this as the only possible judgement and be scandalised in turn.

As they reach top infant level, a wider perspective will be developing for most children. They will be taking more account of others as independent individuals and at the same time most of them will be growing in physical strength and intellectual confidence. This is a time when the peer group can become extremely influential and 'belonging' can be very important.

During the junior years the peer group will remain potentially powerful, although it will not as yet have reached the level of influence that is likely during adolescence. Nor will the peer group embody to any great degree the feeling of separateness from the world at large that is likely to be the case then. As children progress through the junior classes, the basis for fine moral judgement will mature so that factors other than immediate appearances or the teacher's opinion will begin to count.

While age can be an important influence on the way an individual perceives the peer group, the regime in operation can make a difference too. Where the emphasis is on class teaching, the existence of the class as a unit will be underlined throughout the day. The fact that they are addressed as a group, referred to as a group and operate largely as a group will confer a sense of identity on the class and must strengthen the power of the class group in relation to the individual. In a regime that is based on the concept of individualised learning, on the other hand, each child will have more experience of operating on his own or as a member of a small group. The class peer group may therefore be less strong in relation to the individual, although if the small groups remain constant in composition, they may assume alternative strength.

THE CLASS AS PEER GROUP

The power of the class as peer group, whatever the regime and whatever the age of the children concerned, is something which any teacher would be foolish to leave out of account. It is a sort of natural power which operates in two directions at once in the classroom: it has an effect on the individual within it and on the teacher who is outside it. The teacher himself is the major source of power within the classroom and, as always when two power centres exist side by side, they may work in conjunction or in conflict with each other. While there will be brief exceptions, the underlying relationship between the two will tend to be constant once it has become established.

Where conflict becomes the norm in a classroom, it is by no means certain, even in infant classrooms, that the teacher will win. Indeed, when small children are united in their rejection of a teacher, the humiliation may be all the greater. Many a teacher bows to pressure from an obstructive class and leaves the field or hangs on in an unhappy and unproductive situation. The alternative resolution of the conflict, however, is that the teacher dominates an unwilling class and all that remains to be seen of the conflict is an air of sullen or sycophantic fear.

In either case, the experience of the individual child is not a happy one. In the first, he may enjoy the freedom and disorder in the short term or he may feel insecure, but what he will certainly lack is any sense of purpose or fulfilment in his work. In the second case, he will feel dominated and dependent and will most probably conform. Should he choose to rebel, he may find support and protection emanating from the peer group, but if the power of the teacher is sufficiently well established or the teacher is particularly adept at manipulating the peer group, he may find them united in their rejection of him.

Where the teacher works in conjunction with the peer group it is as if he has become an honorary member of the group. Both parties assume an identity of values and purpose and if he is skilful and credible, these will be those of the teacher. For the most part the group will be controlled through this sharing of values, for when the children behave in accord with them, the atmosphere will be pleasantly harmonious, and when they transgress, bonds will be broken and the teacher will no longer be part of the group. This situation of estrangement is likely to prove intolerable to most children and something to be avoided through acceptable behaviour wherever possible.

The individual child in a class where teacher and peer group collaborate can be subject to extremely powerful forces. This can be of enormous benefit to the child who has difficulties, where all combine to help him. It can also assist the teacher in the control of a disruptive individual, where the combined moral pressure of teacher and peer group can prove most effective in persuading him to mend his ways. The other side of the picture, of course, is that in the wrong hands it can provide a powerful means of intimidation of a child who is in any way different from the others. History is full of tyrants who understood well how to manipulate the majority in order to suppress the minority.

THE TEACHER AND THE CLASS

In the early days of their relationship when a class and teacher are settling down together, it is the teacher's actions which are likely to determine whether they settle into a situation of harmony or conflict. This will happen partly through the regime and working conditions which he sets up but most particularly through the way he handles the children generally.

The task can perhaps be viewed as a dual process of both making himself acceptable to the children and making them acceptable to him. As this is achieved, he becomes an honorary member of the peer group.

The qualities which make a teacher acceptable to a class seem to be quite well established over a wide age range of children and in several different countries. They include virtues such as warmth, fairness, firmness, consistency and the ability to communicate. The important thing, of course, is not simply to possess such qualities but to demonstrate them in action with the children. It will make little difference that a young teacher goes home and communicates to his family and friends the extent of his caring if he is cold and unbending when he is actually with the children. If a teacher is to be acceptable he has to convey, through a positive and sustained interest and commitment to the children, the kind of qualities that reassure them.

In turn, the teacher has a right to demand certain qualities from the children which will make them acceptable to him. It is of the utmost importance that he should make it quite clear to the children what these are so that they know what is expected of them.

In many ways, these qualities will mirror their demands on him. He can expect them, for example, to show interest in and concern for each other, to be tolerant and considerate to each other and to outsiders and to be committed to their work. These sorts of values are not difficult to agree for they make life easier for everybody concerned and they may become the agreed ground rules for the peer group–teacher alliance.

The whole process is a circular and continuing one for not only is the alliance based on mutual acceptability but also the maintenance of acceptability depends on the operation of the alliance. How does it all get under way? For the established teacher there is often little difficulty for his reputation will have preceded him and the children will know what to expect. The inexperienced teacher has no such advantage, however, and he needs to be positively demonstrative of the sort of qualities children appreciate right from the beginning. Most primary school children will initially have good expectations even of an unknown teacher. They will expect him to show teacherly qualities and this can provide a breathing space.

Right from the beginning, the new teacher can similarly appear to assume that desirable qualities are present in the children. The important thing is to establish a provisional peer group–teacher alliance which can then sustain itself into a state of permanence.

Initially, the very assumption of an identity of view can help bring all this about. Successful classrooms tend to abound in the early days with phrases such as 'I've heard you're very good at helping each other', 'I know you're good at tidying up', 'I'm surprised you couldn't find anything to do'. The idea of expecting the best and being disappointed when it does not materialise is projected positively right from the start.

Once it is established that the teacher expects the best and is prepared to keep his side of the bargain, the teacher–peer group alliance becomes a reality. The teacher then has a powerful means of managing the children. Group transgressions in the library or misbehaving with another teacher can be treated with the kind of theatrical horror or quiet disillusionment that quickly induces a sense of shame at having failed to live up to expectations. The teacher is temporarily divorced from the group and reconciliation depends on the resolve to improve in the future. Alternatively, the teacher may choose to remain in alliance with the group, accepting some of the blame for their shortcomings and sharing their sense of shame. 'I didn't know what to say when Mrs B. told me how you had behaved in singing. I felt so ashamed.' The incentive then becomes the need to prove that the teacher's faith in the group was really justified and that the present difficulty is an aberration.

THE TEACHER AND THE INDIVIDUAL

The teacher who is accepted by the class group has a powerful weapon to hand for the control of the individual. He can use this power to suppress or to support.

The child who exhibits behaviour considered to be undesirable by the peer group–teacher alliance can be brought under great moral pressure to conform. Where this is aggressive, disruptive, or inconsiderate behaviour which the individual is capable of controlling, then the combined teacher–children force can bring about dramatic reform (see example 1 below). This is particularly so when the child is newly arrived at school, either in reception class or through transfer from another school.

Where the behaviour is a symptom of other difficulties, the child may have little ability to control his actions (example 2). Then the combined force could, in the early stages, achieve little apart from alienating the child and making him very unhappy. Only by sensitive observation of how he reacts is the teacher likely to be able to tell the difference since all kinds of undesirable behaviour seem initially very similar. In cases like these, great care is needed to ensure that the teacher–children alliance does not become simply a destructive force but is also a means of support so that ultimately the child can be helped through his difficulties.

It must be admitted that a strong teacher–children alliance can abuse its power to judge behaviour as undesirable (example 3). If the pack decides to turn on one of its weaker members then the scope for public ridicule and humiliation and for ostracising of the individual is boundless. Fortunately, bullies in the present-day teaching profession are rare. On the other hand, a teacher may protect a child from what might be an adverse judgement by the peer group. A child who arrives with a certain reputation, for example, can be protected from the obligation to live up to it if the teacher appears not to be aware of it (example 4).

The other aspect of teacher–children force is that it enables teacher and children to combine to provide a cradle of support for the individual child who has difficulties to cope with. These may be learning difficulties in which case the group can provide a great deal of practical help and encouragement (example 5). Alternatively, they may be behaviour difficulties, in which case, by showing sympathy (example 6), tolerance (7) and appreciation (8), by making endless allowances and by simply not giving up on the individual, the group can help a child to adjust to trying situations and to build up a degree of confidence or self-control which will stand him in good stead as he grows older.

Where a peer group is able to offer this degree of support to one of its members, it is almost always because a skilful and sensitive teacher is able to form an alliance with the group and to harness its power for the good of the individual. Its power may equally be harnessed for the control of the individual, for good or ill; there may be times when the individual needs protection from it.

A teacher who recognises the potential power of the peer group and uses it effectively has the means to protect and support the individual, to minimise disruptive behaviour and to promote group acceptance for difficult children. He can achieve this by a subtle mixture of approaches. At the same time as tolerance is promoted among the group, more acceptable behaviour is sought from the individual. A request for support for an individual must be accompanied by a rejection of 'typecasting' for that individual. Appreciation of strength goes hand in hand with tolerance of weakness.

Sometimes the teacher will appear as standard setter, sometimes as intermediary; sometimes as possessed of information, sometimes as apparently ignorant. Each case needs to be considered separately and a global approach adopted if the good of the individual is to be served.

(1) Control of disruptive behaviour

At the beginning of the school term after Christmas at Marshlands Primary School, there is a small intake of infants who join one of the two vertically grouped reception and middle infant classes. In their second week they join the other classes for an infant assembly. On this occasion, the head of the infant department was waiting in the large, carpeted music room with her top infant class sitting quietly on the floor providing a model for the younger children. The two vertically grouped classes came in and sat down too. Most of the new children kept a low profile and did what they saw the others do but this seemed to have escaped Jason's notice. He ran in, spotted the piano, dashed over to it, lifted the lid with a clatter and began to 'play a tune'. A scandalised silence greeted his performance. Miss M. looked quizzically at Jason's brother, Mark, who called him to sit beside him. This set Jason off on a run round the outside of the group, watched in horror by the assembled company. Eventually, he realised that nobody was chasing him and came to a halt. Finally, he seemed to become aware that he was alone in his game and that the rest of the company was regarding him with disfavour. 'Come and sit down', said Miss M., holding out her hand to him. 'We're all going to sing a song.' Jason preserved his independence to the extent of ignoring the outstretched hand but he did sit down with the other children. Next time he came into infant assembly, he was happy to observe the conventions of the occasion.

(2) Behaviour which the individual finds it difficult to control
Margaret lived with her father. Her mother left when she was a baby and now, at 8, she was quick tempered and aggressive towards most of the people she met. She was short, stocky, powerful and wore a permanent scowl; she was virtually a non-reader and scarcely able to write. The other children in her class were frightened of her because of the violence which erupted so frequently when she was around so they tended to give her a wide berth. In return, she adopted the attitude of not caring at all about their opinion; instead, she spent as much time as possible with older boys. A state of simmering hostility existed between Margaret and her peer group when they entered Mrs W.'s class. Mrs W. understood that Margaret's experiences of life had probably given her good reason to be angry and realised that to harness the power of the peer group against her would merely drive her into further isolation. She set to work, therefore, to build up a relationship with Margaret herself, encouraging her in her work and finding her things to do to keep her out of trouble. Gradually, she was able to tease her about her scowl and discuss her flaring temper and aggression. There was no miraculous transformation but Margaret did make progress in reading and writing so that she did not appear so exceptional in that respect. She also began to show some signs of attempting to control her own behaviour. Both of these factors helped Mrs W. in her long-term strategy of making Margaret more acceptable to her peer group but it was also as a 'friend' of Mrs W. that they began to accept her. Margaret would never become everybody's favourite person but as the first term wore on the other children did increasingly tolerate her and include her in their plans and there were fewer eruptions.

(3) Abuse of peer group power
Mrs C. had been teaching for many years. She began as a domestic science teacher in a secondary school but found infant teaching more convenient when she had a young family and had remained with the top infant year in a primary school ever since then. Her teaching was

formal and unsuccessful if judged by the children's achievements and the slower children exasperated her. One boy, Michael, particularly infuriated her and she was forever holding up his work as a dreadful warning to the rest of the class. The class obligingly gasped in horror when Michael's hieroglyphics were displayed to them and laughed when Michael's inaccurate responses were recounted to them. Michael would smile diffidently which made Mrs C. crosser than ever. Angela, on the other hand, represented to Mrs C. her credentials as a good teacher. Angela was successful, her writing was neat and lengthy; she could read virtually anything. Her writing was similarly held up and her responses recounted but here the gasps were to be of appreciation. Angela would look gratified and Mrs C. complacent: if Angela could do it, it showed there was nothing wrong with her methods. Both children were rejected by the peer group. Michael was the butt of the children's ridicule as they followed the lead of Mrs C. Angela was the object of jealousy as Mrs C.'s favourite.

(4) Rejection of typing

Jenny was sent to the class halfway through the year as being out of hand and beyond the control of her previous teacher. For the first few days all was peace as the child weighed up the situation, her new teacher, Mrs W., and her new peer group. No mention was made of earlier transgressions and Mrs W. ensured that the work was well within Jenny's capabilities. She also went out of her way to discover wherein Jenny's strengths might lie: she discovered that it was in tidying up that she excelled and allowed her ample opportunity to display these talents. Thus it was with some conviction and credibility that Mrs W. could express disbelief when the first storm broke and Jenny was discovered flicking paint on Melanie's clothes. The peer group, too, was surprised and Jenny was ashamed. Mrs W. was giving her an opportunity to establish herself as a person of merit rather than being typed as 'difficult'. A disruptive act was a matter for surprise rather than expectation. She was also provided with her first insight into the problem of how far the temporary joy of sin compensated for what might be a much more permanent loss of prestige.

(5) Soliciting of assistance

James transferred at the beginning of the top infant year from a school where the policy for reading was *laissez-faire* to one where there was a highly structured approach. He found himself with very little reading ability in a class where even the least able were more advanced than he was. Miss L. saw that there was some danger of James being rejected by the group who had been taught to value reading highly. She therefore arranged for the children to help him wherever possible, encouraging a concern for and pleasure in his progress rather than scorn at his lack of achievement. Since co-operative learning was a feature of the classroom there was little likelihood of patronising attitudes developing. By the first half term, Miss L.'s tutorial efforts combined with the children's assistance had enabled James to achieve a standard of reading in keeping with the conventions of his new class. He and his peer group had arrived at a position of mutual respect and understanding.

(6) Promotion of sympathy

Cathy joined St Chad's halfway through the second term of the third year junior class. Nobody quite knew how many schools she had been to but the number appeared to be approaching double figures. By now she was used to being new to a group and she approached several girls with overtures of friendship but these were rejected because she was not an immediately attractive figure: she was inadequately dressed and washed and she spoke strangely and indistinctly. Moreover, stories abounded in the neighbourhood about the misdoings of her family which had led to the need to move house constantly. Mr T. decided to take an unusual course of action. Normally, he would not speak directly to the class group about an individual for fear that such talk might isolate that child from his peers, but in the case of Cathy, he felt that she was already being cut off so completely that the situation could not be worse. He therefore sent Cathy to the headteacher on some prearranged mission and spoke directly to the class about the unpleasantness of being new, particularly in Cathy's case when it had happened so often, and about responsibilities to a newcomer. Some discussion of the topic followed. In the days after this, Mr T. saw many of the girls making a particular effort to invite Cathy to join in their activities. He knew that their resolution would be short-lived, but by the time it expired Cathy might well have shown herself to be more attractive than was at first apparent and have laid the foundations for friendship.

(7) Promotion of tolerance

Peter was exceedingly fat. When any form of physical education was in progress, there was some danger that his efforts would provoke amusement. Mr K. was in something of a dilemma. If he asked Peter to demonstrate a particular sequence of movements, the amusement was likely to turn to outright laughter. If he never allowed him an opportunity to demonstrate, he would feel that Mr K. valued his efforts less than those of the other children.

His solution was a compromise. Mr K. invited him to perform rather less frequently than the others, thus minimising the opportunity for ridicule. When he did perform, Mr K. alerted the other children to a particular aspect of his work, thus focusing their attention on detail and avoiding the possibly comic overall impression. At the end of his performance, he commented on the effort he had put into the work. Before long, the amusement had been neutralised by this concentration on other aspects of his performance. By arranging the situation to Peter's advantage in this way, the teacher had made it possible for him to achieve a tolerated position amongst his peers.

(8) Promotion of appreciation

Tim had a speech impediment and poor muscular co-ordination. He cried easily and was given to uncontrollable temper tantrums when he was likely to hit out at any child who happened to be near him. He often provoked a great deal of aggressive behaviour in the playground and had to be rescued from taunts and retaliation. He was, however, intelligent, well informed, imaginative, had an unusually wide vocabulary and good use of language. While Miss H. could not do a great deal directly about the situation of the playground, she could ensure conditions where Tim's gifts could be recognised in the classroom. He was given plenty of opportunity to talk and offer ideas and information, and his writing was frequently read out and praised. Gradually, the rest of the class began to appreciate and value what he had to offer. At the same time, Miss H. played down his occasional outbursts, reacting to them as little as possible. Again gradually, the rest of the class began to accept and tolerate his difficulties and ceased to react to them with the same hostility which actions such as his would normally have invoked. By encouraging an appreciation and enjoyment of the things Tim was able to do well, Miss H. ensured that the peer group would not reject him.

Chapter 7

Exceptional Children

While individual children may present a teacher with particular problems, there are also groups of children who might be classed as sharing a common problem. The problem is common in that it may be experienced by several children in a year group but it is also common in that it recurs in a similar form year after year. The most readily recognisable sub-groups of this type are on the one hand the children with learning difficulties and on the other those who achieve exceptionally high standards in their work. While the problems that each group experiences may be fundamentally different, the dangers faced may be similar: circumstances may lead them to become frustrated and to feel increasingly alienated from school. The root of the problem may lie within the child but there is much that the teacher can do to ensure that this does not happen.

Few theorists would quarrel with the notion that performance results from an interaction of ability with maturity and experience and that each of these elements has a vital role to play. Most of us would doubt whether the finest training available in the prime years of our life would have made of us first class sprinters; a certain lack of natural ability precludes this. Attempts to train the exceptionally athletic 5-year-old in pole-vaulting would similarly be doomed to failure in view of his underdeveloped muscle system, and likewise the strong, intelligent 20-year-old would stand little chance in the championship boxing ring unless he had been trained to fight.

While we may recognise the importance of these three factors and agree that exceptionally poor or skilled performance may be due to an outstanding condition of one or all of them, as teachers we know that we can do nothing about a child's natural ability or state of maturity. Experience is the only factor directly accessible to us (although experience may, incidentally, affect the others) so it is here that the positive teacher concentrates his efforts.

It is tempting, when there are thirty or more children in a class to bother about, to leave the gifted child to get on by himself and to put the slow-learning child on one side to mature. Apart from the pressure of time, there is sometimes a feeling that the really bright child will do well, whatever the teacher does, while the really dull child will remain dull, whatever the teacher does.

Such a policy involves an appalling waste of human potential but it is not a very good policy in terms of class control either. The gifted child may well detect that he is being short-changed and create his own diversions to enliven the day and ensure some teacher attention. The slow-learning child is likely to become bored waiting to mature and may seek stimulus outside the official curriculum for which he is made to feel so poorly suited. In both cases, the scene is set for considerable disruptive behaviour.

While a realistic teacher always recognises the limitations of his sphere of influence on a child's learning, he is also conscious of his scope for effectiveness. A wiser policy in the case of exceptional children is to leave no stone unturned in the search for experiences which will motivate them and will fit into and extend the range of abilities which they possess.

Three areas of classroom experience warrant particular attention in this respect. It is more than usually critical that subject matter should be finely matched to the child's level of ability and that the way it is presented should be appropriate, but finally success may depend on the teacher's own attitude and the relationships which he establishes in the class.

THE SLOW-LEARNING CHILD

SUBJECT MATTER

For the slow-learning child the teacher's search will probably be for experiences which enable him to make the most of what ability he has, which may act as a catalyst to lagging development and which will go some way to make up for previous inexperience. Of course, the crucial question is what kind of experiences are appropriate for children who learn slowly?

They must, needless to say, interest and involve children in a positive way. This is not really difficult to achieve as most children are obligingly disposed to be interested in almost anything if it is introduced to them in a way that proclaims it to be interesting. The responsibility for this lies largely with the teacher. Indeed, one of his prime functions is actively to promote enthusiasm rather than leave it to chance, for it is not every day that a butterfly hatches or Tom's brother joins the army, nor every skill that can be taught by means of a dramatic event. Most slow children are quite ready to be made enthusiastic but often their interests and enthusiasm are short-lived and so subject matter may need to be more frequently changed.

While it is not difficult to arouse children's interests, if those interests are to be sustained and long-term learning is to take place, then the subject matter needs to be related to the children and to involve them in an active way. Unfortunately, the phrase 'active learning' often strikes fear into the hearts of those teachers for whom it conjures up images of a seething mass of children all 'doing' something at the same time, but of course the activity may take place in the mind or the imagination and need not involve the limbs. The important thing is that the children should feel that in some way it relates to their own actual or imaginative concerns: learning about Eskimos, for example, can be something of a spectator sport. One of the ways in which the slow child may be slow is in seeing the relevance of what he is learning to his own situation, so the teacher's help here is particularly necessary.

PRESENTATION

Certain methods of presentation to the child with learning problems will be more appropriate than others.

Specificness

The situation needs to be quite specifically geared to the skill to be acquired. If, for example, the object of the exercise is for a child to acquire increased powers of tactile discrimination, it is doubtful whether this will occur if he is merely presented with a table full of bits of material and 'given the opportunity' to feel them. The experience is too wide and too vague for many a slower child. He may do much better with a specific injunction to find suitable materials to cover the cat he has drawn. This will involve him in the more manageable activity of feeling and judging each piece against a recognisable criterion: the furriness of a cat.

Structure

There is a need for much finer structuring of the learning situation than would be necessary with more successful children. In the field of reading, for example, this would imply that phonics would actually be taught rather than left to chance, and that within a phonics programme, each small step would be there for any child who needed it. Intuitively good readers would probably work out for themselves the sound commonly represented by *ea*, particularly once their knowledge of other vowel digraphs led them to expect a long vowel sound. Slower readers might need to be taught every vowel digraph separately before they were able to acquire any degree of fluency.

Repetition

Acquired skills can prove short-lived or of very restricted generality for the slow child unless he is given the opportunity to repeat them in as many varied situations as possible. The child learning to count, for example, will probably need to fill a box with five marbles, a bottle with five sticks, his pocket with five sweets, thread five beads on a string, and so on, in innumerable situations before he has any permanent grasp of the unchanging nature of five.

Explicitness
Ideas need to be well discussed and overtly expressed with the child being guided quite some way along the road to drawing his own conclusions. A discussion of second marriages, for example, might be necessary before a slow child understood the motivation of Snow White's stepmother. If too much is left unspoken, he may draw the wrong conclusions. This is particularly so in the case of vocabulary, with often unintentionally hilarious results.

ATTITUDES

A most important feature in the school experience of any child but particularly in that of the slow-learning child is the attitude of the teacher himself. If he expects little of the children he teaches, then this is what he will tend to get. If he is over-impressed by a disadvantaged home background, for example, he may in the very anticipation of low achievement set up the conditions to ensure it. If he is convinced that a child is prevented by limited ability from ever being successful, he may be so concerned to protect him from failure that he never even offers him the opportunity to try.

The teacher who aims to take every child as far as he can go will have a positive, planned approach and an end in view. He will not set the slow-learning child aside to 'mature', he will not postpone structured learning situations for him while he force-feeds him with 'enriching experiences', he will not expect less than he can give because 'he hasn't got much'. Of course, the task must fit the child, but there must be a task; a child with learning problems is unlikely to make much progress if he spends large sections of the day crayoning pictures or playing with plasticine when others have work to do.

THE GIFTED CHILD

SUBJECT MATTER

With gifted children the teacher's aim will be to set up experiences which not only provide meat for intellectual growth but also contribute to the child's all-round development. Sometimes very able children experience a sort of lop-sided development. It may be, for example, that his intellectual development outstrips his social development. Then there could be a need for the deliberate fostering of social contact: compensation is not the exclusive preserve of the underprivileged.

Selection of subject matter is particularly important with the gifted child for he is likely to be more discriminating about what he allows himself to become involved in. A teacher may have to search harder for areas that will interest him. On the other hand, the child himself is more likely to have interests of his own which he will share with the teacher. These interests may well be of a longer duration than is usual with children of his age group. This means, of course, that he needs to be allowed to carry on with them for longer spells of time though others may have changed to quite different activities; a flexible organisation allows this to happen quite easily.

In the infant years, it may well be that the exceptionally able child feels that he has exhausted the possibilities of some of the play areas at a time when the other children are still happily engrossed. He may be demanding activities which have more of the appearance of formalised work. There are two lines of action which the teacher may take here. One is to accept this development and allow such a child to undertake the activities he prefers. The other is to extend his concept of what is possible in the play areas through suggesting alternative activities, providing additional equipment or novel arrangements, or through the restructuring of groups.

PRESENTATION

One of the problems for the teacher of gifted children is to plan rewarding learning experiences for them and to take account of the competing demands of the rest of the class at the same time.

Techniques

It is a worthwhile investment of time to teach the gifted child techniques which may not be within the grasp of others in his group but which may give him the key to further independent learning. An early introduction to reference work, for example, can open to him an unlimited world of experience in books. Well-developed recording skills in mathematics enable him to demonstrate solutions to problems of his own devising.

Materials

Whenever a sequence of work-cards is being prepared, it pays to include a few extra cards at the top end which would be geared exclusively to the gifted child, carrying him further along the line than would be deemed appropriate for most. If the basic fraction pack deals with $\frac{1}{2}$, $\frac{1}{4}$ and $\frac{1}{3}$, the extra cards could progress to $\frac{1}{32}$. If most cards require the reading ability of an 8-year-old, the extra ones could demand a reading age of 11.

Questions
A skilful teacher always has an additional question ready for the exceptional child. Sometimes this may set him off on a whole new line of activity: if a group of children have been studying staff travel to school, he may be asked how much petrol he would need if he used a Mini to collect each member of staff in turn – an exercise involving him in several additional operations for the small price of a moment of teacher time.

Opportunism
It is often easier to capitalise on opportunity with the gifted child than with others. A foreign coin may signify little but novelty of shape and lettering to most children. To the exceptional child it may prove to be an imaginative introduction to the study of a foreign country.

ATTITUDES

One of the most difficult things for us to adjust to as teachers is the knowledge that we are teaching people who are more able than we are. Gifted children do occasionally suffer on account of the feelings of insecurity they engender in their teachers but in the main this is something which teachers come to terms with early in their career, safe in the knowledge that in the primary school years at least the superiority is potential rather than actual.

There is, nevertheless, still one overriding problem in dealing with gifted children and this is the treading of the knife edge between special provision and preferential treatment. Exceptions must be made for the exceptional child, if he is to be given full opportunity to develop. Yet any hint of exclusiveness can saddle a young child with an arrogant preciousness which it may take him years to shake off. In the meantime, he may have to lead a somewhat isolated existence, distrusted by his peers, particularly if he is blossoming in an inner city school.

The flexible grouping advocated previously may go some way towards guarding against this sense of specialness. The chief protection lies, however, in the atmosphere of the class generally. The important thing is to foster a respect for all manner of gifts and skills, even that of being able to cross one's eyes at will; a tacit appreciation of achievement in relation to ability, even when the child to be praised for receiving his first reading book is 7 years old; and a sense of mutual responsibility, even though you would rather drink your milk than look for Raymond's vest for the third time this week. This sense of belonging to a caring and appreciative community is as important to the gifted child as to any other and may in his case help him to preserve a sense of perspective.

Dealing with exceptional children is never easy, even in schools or classes which cater exclusively for them. In the context of ordinary classes, they constitute particularly difficult sub-groups. Attempts to merge them into the rest of the class and deny their special needs will certainly do little to help the children themselves and may ultimately lead to an explosive situation which may make the class as a whole difficult to handle. The only solution lies in recognising the problem and on the one hand planning special learning experiences, and on the other expecting them to operate as fully committed members of the class group, sharing the standards and values of the class as a whole.

Chapter 8

Coping with Problem Children

When we talk about coping with behaviour problems we generally assume that the chief aim is to help children adjust to the school society in which they find themselves: to get the withdrawing child to engage in more active commerce with others, and to get the attention-seeking child to allow the limelight to fall on someone else. We accept, at least tacitly, that in pursuit of this aim we shall be urging children towards the mean, encouraging retiring children to come forward, and forward children to retire. In doing so we are only extending the pattern that operates in life outside school, but we should recognise what we do in order that we guard against pressurising children into over-conformity, and that we ensure that the school society is worth adjusting to; there is no reason why we should expect children to conform in a society that is uncongenial to the majority of them.

The teacher's role in helping children to come to terms with their problems is critical, first, because it is his job to ensure that the class society is one to which they actively want to belong, and secondly, because there is so much he can do, in the way he handles children and in the way he manipulates the conditions, to make it easier for the problem child to adjust.

Of course, the teacher's role can also be critical in helping to create maladjustment. A noisy, disorganised and aimless classroom, for example, will be an unrewarding place for most and acceptance within it will therefore not constitute a goal for children in that class. Equally, there are teachers who intuitively handle children in such a way as to provoke problem behaviour. Particularly damaging are those who are not prepared to adapt to the needs of the individual, who operate on an eye for an eye basis, who manage to be at one and the same time inflexible and unfair and who are not willing to put in the enormous amount of time and effort that is necessary to cope with difficult children. Indeed it seems possible for teachers and even schools as a whole to act as manufacturers of maladjustment. Children who were without problems acquire them under their regime.

On the other hand, there are teachers and schools who are able to make it seem as if they have no children at all with problems. Some teachers seem to perform an annual miracle; they take a rather unlikeable class full of difficult children and transform it into an eager group with a strong sense of identity and no problems that cannot be coped with.

It is a most encouraging sight but how is this miracle achieved? One of the factors seems to be the ability to distinguish between fundamental problems and passing difficulties, particularly with young children. The infant school years are a time of very rapid development and a time when new demands are made on children. Many behaviour problems seem to be chiefly a product of this swift movement and really will just go away if treated with patience. The child who feels himself to have made great intellectual progress may not have matured sufficiently socially or emotionally to cope with it: a time of intolerable arrogance may ensue but patience on the part of adults will generally see a decline to a more realistic self-assessment. The child who is frightened and withdraws from any degree of undressing for PE will generally become accustomed to the idea as he sees others doing it. If a teacher sets out to 'solve' such situations forcibly, she may well create more problems than she removes.

Nevertheless, there are enduring problems which cannot be left to go away and this is where the conditions that the skilled teacher creates and the action that he takes in relation to the individual combine to create that miracle of transformation.

The child with behaviour problems often has something in his background that makes us, as teachers, feel tremendously sorry for him. Perhaps his mother has left him, his father is a bully, he is inadequately fed and clothed, he is left alone at night, he carries the major work load of the household. It is not surprising when circumstances like these lead to problem behaviour and it is tempting to let our sympathy take over and allow complete licence to a child in such difficulties.

Yet to do so merely compounds his problems, adding yet another handicap. Outlandish behaviour is likely to cause immediate unhappiness and if he cannot live reasonably with other people, then his chances of ultimate happiness are slim too. Apart from these considerations, there are many kinds of behavioural difficulty which it would be unrealistic to attempt to leave unchecked, for the effect on others in the class would be unfair. This is particularly so with aggressive children.

It is also tempting in such instances to express our sympathy directly and to attempt to talk about the home problem. But for many children, this is disturbing. It invites confidences which they may not be prepared to give and which they would regard as disloyal. It may also disturb their notion of what a teacher–pupil relationship should properly be, namely, that the teacher is there to help them learn. Communication is more likely to be established through the job that teacher and child are there to do. Connie Rosen (1967) expresses it well:

> I can only aim at making a triangle of myself, the children and the activities outside both of us, but in which we are both involved for different reasons . . . In the course of such activities, I would hope to build a relationship where they would feel safe to talk about anything that concerned them.

As time goes by, it may become possible to talk directly about background problems, but in the meantime, sympathy and concern can be expressed with great clarity in the degree of interest and care that is given to the work that the child does and more practical help can often be contrived impersonally. The ingenious teacher can devise ways of ensuring that a child receives a packet of crisps or warm, second-hand clothing without being apparently involved in the distribution himself.

Of course, not talking about background and personal problems is not the same as not talking about behavioural problems. There is often much to be gained by bringing unacceptable behaviour out into the open and discussing it with the child as a problem to which a solution must be found. In the same way, progress towards that solution can be examined regularly.

Unless the relationship between a teacher and a child is right, it is unlikely that much progress will be made. It has been suggested that relationships are established in the common ground of learning activities. In the case of a child with behaviour problems, there are frequently also learning problems. Whichever class of problems arose first, it is certain that the two interact and that each exacerbates the other. It becomes doubly critical, therefore, to ensure that the problem child experiences satisfaction in the learning activities which the teacher devises for him. Perhaps it is that these must be sufficiently taxing to make demands on a child who has found things contemptibly easy hitherto. More often it is a case of finding work which will provide the experience of success for a child who is more accustomed to failure.

As well as being matched to the ability level of the learner, it is important that the work should engage his interest. It is not uncommon for children to decide, quite early in their school career, that nothing they are required to do relates to anything that they are really interested in. Nor are the activities those which they enjoy and are good at. If their enthusiasm can once be rekindled, it often becomes possible to hook them back on the learning system.

Providing interesting work at the right level of difficulty prepares the ground for another of the necessary conditions for success with many problem children, that is, the promotion of confidence. Many problem children lack confidence not only in themselves but also in their teachers. To find yourself actually enjoying work is a great boost to the morale; if you can do that, who knows what is possible? Moreover, a teacher who can achieve this may well be able to achieve some of those other miracles which his manner suggests. Present success justifies optimism for the future and breaks the cycle of frustration.

So far this all sounds very serious, but perhaps one of the most important requirements for dealing with problem children is a sense of humour. This is necessary for the teacher who might become overwhelmed by the private tragedy that surrounds many of these children or explode with the frustration of dealing with them, if he were not able to distance himself sufficiently to see the funny side of many of their antics. While it is very naughty of a child to stuff crayons up his nose or eat paste, it is also undeniably amusing. Equally, if a child can be brought to see the funny side of his own unintentionally amusing behaviour he has taken the first step towards being able to take an objective view of himself, an ability singularly lacking in many problem children.

Having ensured that the working conditions are conducive to helping children to come to terms with their problems, it is necessary to construct a policy for handling each child. This must certainly be set within the context of the peer group for, as has already been discussed, this is one of the major resources for the teacher dealing with individuals with difficulties. In addition, account must be taken of the parents, whose supportive role is also discussed in greater detail elsewhere. It must be said, however, that many difficult children have difficult parents who may be either unwilling or unable to provide the help that is needed and may indeed themselves be part of the problem for the child. An aggressive father, for example, stands every chance of producing either an aggressive or particularly timid son. Equally surely, an overprotective mother is likely to produce a child who finds it difficult to adjust to school and may be very unhappy in the early days.

Unwilling parents can often be persuaded to become concerned by a direct appeal from the school. Sometimes a way of talking about a parent's own role in the problem can be found, and it may be that the headteacher himself will undertake this task if the teacher is very young or inexperienced. Certainly, it is worth making every effort to involve parents as at the very least this removes the classic rebellious child's weapon, 'I'll bring my Dad'. Nevertheless, it is often the case, with problem children, that they receive help in school in spite of their parents.

Against this complex background of school and home, what kind of positive help can be offered to each individual child? While problems and children are all different, there are certain principles which can be applied in all cases.

The first of these is that it is important to be both consistent and persistent. The child needs to know that you will make it clear what is expected of him and what the limits are; that your standards will not vary from one area of school life to another or from one day to the next; that you will be invariably fair in your dealings with him; in other words, that you can be relied upon to declare the rules of the game and not then to change them. He also needs to realise that you will not give up, however much easier that might be. This may involve, at certain periods of time, being on hand almost every moment of the day: before school begins, at playtime, at dinner-time as long as may be necessary to establish new patterns of behaviour. Even though you might compromise, you will never just let things go. A corollary of this is that you will never just let him go as a hopeless case.

The second principle is that if, as is often the case, a situation of confrontation seems ultimately likely to arise, the teacher should choose the time and the terms. A sensitive teacher can predict most of the situations which could lead to confrontation and can take steps to avoid such an outcome. As with income tax, avoidance is not the same as evasion: stepping out of the way of something is different from hiding from it. In the case of the problem child, the skilful teacher anticipates trouble and diverts the child from the path of confrontation rather than allowing it to happen and then giving in.

Postponement of confrontation will achieve two things. It will give the child a sense of what it is like to lead a battle-free life. The longer this goes on, the more he will have to lose by confrontation. It will also enable the teacher to prepare the ground for a show-down if this appears inevitable. He can explain his tactics to the child's parents, he can get to know the child well enough to decide how best to deal with him and he can choose the time and the place most advantageous to himself. If confrontations have to happen, it is important that the teacher should win.

The third principle is that if the child is entrenched in a situation of behavioural failure, that situation should be in some way changed. The degree of change can vary from the cosmetic to the radical, but in some way a fresh start will be available and an implicit reason for past failure and future improvement will be provided.

What kind of change is it feasible to make? Some changes would involve a school rather than a class policy. If a child has really reached breakdown point in his own class, it could be worthwhile to transfer him to another class where he starts afresh with a new teacher who may adopt a different perspective on his problem, and with a new peer group with whom he may have a chance to live down his reputation.

Less drastic but sometimes equally effective is a change of

friendship group. While teachers clearly cannot pick children's friends for them, they can create the conditions in which friendship may flourish. An alteration in seating arrangements or an allocation of shared responsibility for a task such as counting the crisp money can bring children together and could provide friends for lonely children or more stable company for children with a penchant for trouble.

Having a job can, in itself, make a difference for a child with problems. The awareness of trust and responsibility can do a lot for the child with damaged self-respect and the actual location of the task can ensure that he either is somewhere where it is advantageous for him to be or is not somewhere where he may get into situations which it may be hard for him to cope with.

Seating arrangements also in themselves offer scope for useful change. A child who is a hardened distractor of other children and who is himself distracted very easily can often benefit from a period of solitary confinement as close to the teacher as possible. It is amazing how much more work gets done when there is really no alternative.

A child who has become quite overwhelmed with a problem can often be helped if that problem is removed and broken down into such small parts that they appear to bear little resemblance to the original problem. This is particularly so where a child has developed a phobia about some aspect of school life such as eating his dinner. If he can be persuaded merely to sit at the table with no compulsion to eat, a start will have been made along the road to solving the problem.

Often the change may be in the behaviour of the teacher himself: an unexpected reaction to a disruptive incident may jolt the offender out of his customary pattern of offences. The child who has been used to a shocked reaction may be disconcerted by a teacher who appears unimpressed. An ominously quiet tone or a dramatic shout in a usually peaceful atmosphere may both shake the nerve of a brazen wrongdoer. Equally disturbing may be a joke reaction on the teacher's part: he may imitate the child's own behaviour, for example, and this can appear so innately ridiculous that the situation is immediately defused. At the same time, attention-seeking behaviour which is ignored loses its *raison d'être*; true, a teacher cannot turn his back on everything but there are many types of histrionics which can be safely left to play themselves out.

There is an immense variety of techniques which a teacher can use to change the situation for the child in some way. Some he may use intuitively, others he may build into his policy quite deliberately. None will work in the long term, however, unless they are set against a background of rewarding experience for the child within the classroom generally. Really effective help for children with behaviour problems requires an immensely subtle orchestration of environment and events.

Finally, it would be misleading to suggest that all problems can be resolved once and for all by a teacher's skill in handling the situation. Some problems are so fundamental that they cannot be radically relieved within the school. The effect of particularly adverse family circumstances or gross personality disorders cannot be removed as if by magic. But almost always, complete breakdown can be avoided and some progress can be made by the teacher who is sufficiently wily and tenacious.

Kevin

When Kevin joined Miss D.'s third year junior class, he had a reputation for being obstructive and aggressive. He was physically well built, with close-cropped hair and he always wore heavy boots; indeed, he looked like a miniature Bill Sykes and was fond of adopting a threatening manner with other children, though he was seldom actually involved in physical hostilities. This may have been because the other children mostly backed down. He often refused to work and consequently did very little. Miss D. was inexperienced and it took her a little time to realise that Kevin was not being unco-operative when he refused to do things but that he genuinely found them too difficult. He was having a great deal of trouble with Gay Way's red lorry and all its pots and pans. She also began to suspect that much of his aggression was bravado. She adopted a new approach to reading and devised work for him which was within his capabilities. Often it was necessary to work with him before school began but gradually he began to make progress and to experience pride in his own achievements. For a while, Miss D. made him responsible for keeping the class library tidy, partly to keep him away from trouble in the playground and partly to ensure that there was a reason for him to be around at unusual times so that his need for remedial help should not be too conspicuous. In the course of all this, the soft side of Kevin emerged which was very much at odds with his appearance. He completely abandoned refusing to do things and his aggressiveness reduced considerably, although it was too much a part of his image for it to disappear completely. He never became a fluent reader but he learned to cope with print well enough to maintain appearances. The other children gradually realised that in spite of his tough exterior he was not a violent boy; on the contrary, he was quite generous in his relationships and could often be relied upon to provide moral protection for the less robust in the class.

Edward

Edward was one of the youngest of a large family, all of whom had passed through Clifton Street Primary School. The family name was distinctive and appeared regularly in the local newspaper in connection with a variety of crimes ranging from drunkenness and petty theft to prostitution. No teacher could be unaware of the reputation enjoyed by the family and Edward certainly set about justifying it from the moment he entered Mr Y.'s first year junior class. He was small, neat and nimble. He possessed the ability to disappear from one side of the classroom and materialise at the other without ever being seen to move; the transposition seemed to satisfy his constant desire for change. His chief aim in school was apparently to astound people and since he could not achieve this through physical strength or academic prowess, he resorted to daring. Edward did things that other children did not dare to do. At the beginning of the year, Mr Y. was determined not to let Edward's family reputation influence him unduly and tried to maintain a balanced and impartial attitude, leaning over backwards to be fair and make allowances for him. Eventually, however, he had to admit to himself that Edward was indeed a naughty boy and give some thought as to how best to deal with him. He decided to ignore his outrageous behaviour as far as possible and look for ways in which Edward could more acceptably impress other members of the class. Often Edward's behaviour was not easy to ignore. Mr Y. had difficulty himself in not laughing when he caught sight of a table moving steadily across the back of the classroom without apparent human agency, although the sight of Edward hanging upside down from the top of the window frame was less amusing. Nevertheless, he succeeded and through his own force of influence with the rest of the class he managed to persuade the other children largely to ignore Edward too. This was very frustrating to Edward who became more and more exhibitionist in his behaviour. One day, when Edward began to hurl verbal abuse at him, Mr Y. stopped the class, called Edward out to the front and told him to go ahead and impress them all. Edward was disconcerted at being given the stage in this way: being offered attention was less satisfying than seeking it and he did not know what to do with it. For a while he quietened down, and Mr Y. used the opportunity to involve him in intensive athletics training. Soon, Edward began to build up a reputation as one of the best short-distance runners the school was likely to have; teachers and children alike were astonished at his turn of speed. Edward's need to amaze by other means decreased (although it never disappeared completely!) and when he discovered a facility, encouraged by Mr Y. for entertaining people by telling jokes, the need declined still further. Edward remained unpredictable throughout the year but as time went by he developed the ability to keep his exhibitionism just within the bounds of acceptability.

Josephine

Josephine was a very quiet child. Indeed, there were days when Mr A. was scarcely aware that she was there at all. Her mother brought her to school every morning and afternoon and collected her at the end of each session, although this was unusual for a second year junior child. Mr A. did not worry unduly about this because, although Josephine never initiated contact with him, she was always quite happy to talk to him if he started the conversation and he observed that she communicated quite freely with her small group of friends in the class. Halfway through the year, however, he began to receive frequent visits from Josephine's mother to explain that she would not be coming to school because she had something wrong with her. The range and regularity of the minor illnesses made him uneasy about the child and he asked the headteacher to talk to her mother about it as he did not want to compromise his position as a sympathetic teacher by revealing his scepticism. Josephine's mother showed herself to be concerned, too, about the child's frequent illness but agreed that she had a tendency to worry too much. This she explained was probably because she had lost her first child with pneumonia in its infancy. She agreed to try to bring Josephine in every day unless she actually had a temperature. Mr A. decided that he must tackle the problem from the other direction and make Josephine actively want to come into school rather than yield to her mother's protective urgings. He decided to mount a class entertainment for the rest of the school hoping that Josephine would get caught up in the feeling of solidarity that arises from being involved in a production. He had in mind a non-speaking role but one of her friends suggested to him that she would make a good queen. He was amazed when she agreed to try and even more amazed when he found that she was a natural actress. He had discovered an activity to involve her positively and at last to give her scope for expression just where he least expected it. As Josephine's commitment to the class increased so her willingness to stay away declined. At the same time, the headteacher kept a watchful eye on her mother ensuring that she stuck to her agreement to bring Josephine to school regularly.

Sarah

Sarah caused so much trouble in her second year infant class that she was moved up to Top Infants a term early. Both she and her mother were convinced that she was very able and surrounded by foolish children and an inadequate teacher who did not appreciate her; this lack of appreciation led to great frustration and uncontrollable temper tantrums involving aggression towards other children and much tears and sobbing. In reality, she was an able enough child but her work was not exceptional, as she never seemed to commit herself to it entirely. When she joined the new class there was no longer any question of superiority to the other children who were older than her, and the new teacher was Miss P., an experienced and well-respected teacher who was deputy head of the school. Miss P. decided that the first thing to do was to keep very close tabs on Sarah to make sure that she worked to capacity. She therefore ensured that Sarah always sat where she could be observed closely, that there was always plenty for her to do at the right level of difficulty and that she herself was always on hand to make certain that she did it and to defuse any potentially disturbing situation. There was a period of tranquility while Sarah kept a relatively low profile, confining her aggression to poking children from time to time. The other children regarded her warily. The day came, however, as Miss P. knew it would, when something thwarted Sarah and she could contain herself no longer. Suddenly the room was filled with screams, shouts and the stamping of feet as abuse was hurled at all those within range. Miss P., normally a very quietly spoken teacher, went over to Sarah, put her face very close to hers and shouted at her. She told Sarah that she had best stop that noise because no one would take any notice of her until she did. Everybody then got on with what they were doing and gradually Sarah tired herself out. Eventually she was able to rejoin the group where she was just quietly accepted by Miss P. Later the child and the teacher were able to talk about the problem and make plans to prevent it recurring. Of course it did recur, but far less often than previously. Gradually, the new group accepted her and when her old group caught her up the following term, she was able to occupy a position of genuine prestige as someone who knew the ropes and coped with difficult work. With so much at stake, she grew more and more able to control her outbursts.

Matthew

Matthew was first brought to St Albert's by the educational welfare officer. He had been failing to attend Larkhill Road with any degree of regularity and had recently been found frequenting the men's toilets in the town centre when his mother assumed him to be at school. She was worried about him, particularly as one of his older sisters was already appearing in court, charged with shoplifting, and the other had got so beyond her control that she had had to be sent to live with her grandmother. Mother felt the home was falling apart, father having long since disappeared without trace. The headteacher at St Albert's was sympathetic to the situation and was fortunately able to place Matthew in a class with one of the most sensitive teachers in the school. Together, they made school life for him as pleasant and interesting as possible. He was encouraged and reassured at every opportunity and soon he began to improve what was initially a very poor level of academic achievement. After a while, however, his attendance became erratic and the headteacher called in the educational welfare officer. He reported that things had gone from bad to worse at home. Matthew's mother had taken to drink and was frequently in no state to get him to school at all. The older sister had been put into care so that Matthew was now the only child at home and he appeared to resent the fact that his mother was drunk and incapable for so much of the time. As often as possible after this, somebody from the school called to collect Matthew when he did not appear but sometimes the door was not opened. The sisters ran away and returned to their home town from time to time and Matthew would then fail to come to school for several days, preferring to spend his time with them. The school recognised that there was nothing that they could do which they could be sure would improve his home circumstances and that there would be no happy ending to Matthew's story for many years to come. The best they could do was to get him to school as often as they could and make life as rewarding as possible while he was there.

David

David was in the third year of the junior school when he developed the habit of slipping away from school during the afternoon playtime. For some time, this was not noticed. If his teacher, Mr S., became aware at all that David was not in class, he assumed that he was doing something with the headteacher. Things came to a head one day when his mother called for him unexpectedly at home-time. A search was instituted and eventually he was tracked down waiting on the doorstep at home. The following day, both parents came in to see the headteacher and report on the inquest which they had conducted the previous evening. Evidently, David had said that he always left at playtime and then waited at the end of his street until it was time for him to come home. The reason he gave was that he was afraid to come away from school at the same time as everybody else in case he 'got beaten up'. To begin with Mr S. and the headteacher thought that this would not be a difficult problem to deal with. They delivered stern warnings to the boys that David seemed to regard as potential assailants and looked for someone else who followed the same route home so that they could arrange for company for David. Here the first difficulty arose. No-one lived on the same route. Mr S. was not unduly concerned, however, as he felt that now that everything was out in the open and the dangers of attack dealt with, David's fears would evaporate and he would be able to follow a normal home-time routine. Unfortunately, it transpired that David's fears had reached phobic proportions and he seemed quite incapable of conforming. A difficult few days followed when both Mr S. and the headteacher spent the last session of the afternoon jumping every time they heard a door open, creeping nervously up and down corridors and stairs and loitering nonchalantly outside the boys' cloakroom. Again and again, David eluded them and he seemed to develop a sense of despair at his own behaviour. Between them Mr S. and the headteacher worked out a plan of action. First, David was appointed to a newly created position together with the most good-natured and reliable boy in his class. Each afternoon playtime they were to tidy up the science equipment. At the end of playtime, they were to bring either the headteacher or Mr S. to check their work. This would then enable the person concerned to accompany them back to the classroom and ensure that at least David was present at the beginning of the last session. Secondly, he was not to be allowed to leave the room until five minutes before the end of school when he would be sent down to the headteacher's room. When it was exactly home-time, the headteacher would let him out of the back door and watch him to the end of the street where his mother would meet him. This highly defined approach seemed to reassure David and he found that he could keep to the conditions laid down. Gradually, his enjoyment of his job and a growing friendship with his co-worker began to obscure his worries at playtime, and little by little the home-time props were reduced – the headteacher began simply to let him out and not watch him, his mother gradually reduced the distance she came along his route, he began to use the same door as everyone else. By a series of stages, he finally reached the point where no special arrangements were necessary, although Mr S. never lost the habit of keeping a special eye on him for the last part of the afternoon.

Chapter 9

Adults in the School

While we tend to think of teachers as the principal adults in primary schools, in reality they are only part of the adult work force of most schools. All schools will have a caretaker and probably cleaners, most will have a secretary, women to serve and possibly cook the dinners, welfare assistants to look after the children at dinner-time and, if they are really lucky, ancillary assistants to help with routine classroom preparation. In addition, there will be regular visits to the school from such people as the priest, the nurse and the welfare officer.

A varied collection of people like this represents such a wealth of experience and such a range of different personalities that they constitute a tremendous resource, particularly for a small primary school. Most will have chosen and been chosen for their jobs because they have an interest in children. Many of them are themselves parents. Most of them, unlike teachers, could be doing their jobs in a completely different setting so it is significant that they have chosen to do them in schools. Yet many schools fail to take advantage of the opportunities that their presence offers and may even find them an additional difficulty to cope with rather than a source of assistance.

There may be many reasons for this and often these are centred on differences in management style. Non-teaching adults may have different ways of addressing children and of relating to them which may not fit in with school policy on such matters. Some teachers may feel sufficiently insecure in their role to feel threatened by the idea of other adults being involved in the education of the children in their charge. Yet involved they are, and the wise teacher can turn this factor to his children's advantage. Indeed, it seems foolish not to ensure that other adults contribute to the life of the school in the most positive way possible.

Clearly all of them do contribute simply in the way that they do their jobs. Together they provide a clean, safe and well-serviced environment for the children. Often they are happy to contribute more than this on a purely practical level. Many is the time that a caretaker makes sets of bookshelves, a secretary types up children's poems, a cook makes biscuits for the Christmas party and welfare assistants help create the costumes for a school play. Services such as these can oil the wheels of school life considerably.

Beyond this kind of practical help, however, there are other ways in which they have much to contribute. First of all, they are a source of interest and information, not only in relation to the jobs they do but also in relation to their own hobbies and interests. If a child is trying to find out about something which has caught his attention, it is often possible to find someone among the extended adult work force of the school who has particular knowledge of the area. A caretaker who is expert at morse code, a secretary who teaches flower-arranging at night school, a welfare assistant who can crochet the most elaborate patterns, a nursery assistant who works closely with a group of physically handicapped: none of these is an unusual skill or interest but all might remain unnoticed if the professional staff took no steps to discover them.

Even in the roles for which they are known in school, however, there is great educational potential. So often we search for real situations and first-hand experience which can provide stimulus and input for children, but here is a rich seam of reality which often goes untapped. All adults in the school can provide the subject matter for children conducting interviews, drawing up reports and painting pictures. In the process, the children will learn a great deal about what is involved in the work that the adults do and the adults will develop more understanding of the work that the children do.

Perhaps the most continuing contribution that the non-teaching adults have to make, however, is that of being surrogate parent in the school. To a degree it could be argued that this is what teachers are, but there are important differences. Non-teaching adults do not have responsibility for children's learning, nor for the control of children *en masse*. They relate to them individually and in small groups as would be the case in the home; they are not required to teach them anything and are therefore free of the possible background tensions that that implies.

This leaves them free to lend a sympathetic ear to problems that a child may not feel able to discuss with the teacher. But in other ways it means that they are able to complement the work of the teacher just as parents do. We know that conversation with adults is important to the language development of children, yet pressure of numbers inevitably limits the amount of exchange between teachers and individual children. There are many opportunities for them to converse with other adults in the school. Children with a newly acquired skill enjoy rehearsing it for the benefit of others. They like saying tables to adults, for example. Children who need practice at a certain level will often coerce others into helping; they will read to anybody who will listen. There are many ways in which children will learn from adults without being taught.

The fact that the potential of non-teaching adults in a school is seldom fully exploited may not be entirely the fault of the teaching staff, for it would be unrealistic to suggest that all non-teaching adults would agree to being involved in the ways discussed and it is easy in any case to overestimate the time at their disposal. But if they do want to be involved as fully as possible, there seems no reason why the problem should not be tackled head-on. The headteacher could discuss ways of handling children with each newly appointed adult. He could explain the work of the school more fully and show what teachers were trying to achieve when they did certain things and how non-teaching adults could help in quite incidental ways. Perhaps from time to time a meeting could be held of all staff, both teaching and non-teaching. Measures like this help to promote a sense of involvement and a greater appreciation of possibilities.

They also prepare the way for particular arrangements between teachers and non-teachers. Sometimes it helps for the caretaker to be aware of a difficulty being experienced by an individual child, for example. He may be able to involve him in activities which are not within the range of the teacher but will ease him through the problem: a spell of painting storage boxes alongside a male caretaker could help the boy with an absentee father. The secretary and the welfare assistants can provide a tremendous boost in a short period of time for the child who has made a breakthrough in reading and has an insatiable desire to read to someone. This is useful support for the teacher who is looking to create optimal learning situations for children.

It may be a good idea, too, to compile a resource list with contributions from all adult staff and regular visitors to the school who agree. This would consist of areas of interest and abilities which could be called upon by individuals or groups of children in the course of their school work. All adults would simply be invited to disclose their skills and enthusiasms, although there need be no pressure on those who were unwilling. Not only would such a resource list be a useful source of information but it might also lead to greater mutual appreciation.

Adults who are professionally involved in a school are not the only adults concerned with the school, however. Parents also have a legitimate right to be deeply involved in school affairs. We have plenty of evidence now to suggest that positive parental support for and interest in their children's education is markedly associated with positive achievement on the children's part. The obvious conclusion is that the more parental interest and support that can be aroused, the better it will be for the children. Certainly, the Plowden Report made a strong plea for schools to regard it as their responsibility to keep parents informed about the school itself and their children's progress and to involve parents in out-of-school activities. Since then, it has become the practice in many primary schools to go further than this and to involve parents in the day-to-day activities of the schools. Where this brings them to work inside the classroom on a regular basis, it may make for difficulties with many teachers who do not feel comfortable working side-by-side with parents.

Those who do feel this reluctance tend to be apologetic about it and to feel themselves professionally lacking when they confess to it. Yet it is a totally understandable reaction. The presence of parents in a classroom undoubtedly can bring problems. The children may be tempted to show off. The parents may acquire knowledge of other people's children which they may not use discreetly. The teacher may feel inhibited in the way that he deals with children, partly because a new factor has been added to a carefully balanced equation of relationships, and partly because few people, including parents, like to be observed when they exercise authority. Certainly, it has been argued throughout this book that effective child management arises from consistency of handling and control of the working environment. Parents in the classroom can make it very difficult to operate such a policy.

The difficulties are not insuperable, however. Some teachers accommodate extremely well to the presence of parents and find them an invaluable source of help with many of the routine tasks of the classroom, and in some situations where the individual attention of an adult is crucial. Equally, some parents quickly adapt to and enjoy a discreet and semi-professional role. Where this is the case, the interests of both parent and teacher are served.

It is unfair for this idyllic state of affairs to be held up as a model to which all should aspire, however. It is not the only way of interesting and involving parents in their children's education and indeed may be one of the least effective ways in terms of the numbers of parents which it is practicable to include in such arrangements. Open days, interviews, booklets, reports, curriculum evenings, parent support groups, help with out-of-school activities, help outside the classroom, home visits, home tasks - all of these arrangements may lead to that close involvement of parents which research has shown to be vital. They can prove a useful supplement to the considerable amount of informal contact that teachers and parents have every day when children are brought to and collected from school, particularly in the younger classes.

The important thing is that the school should make itself comprehensible and accessible to parents. It is not necessary for parents to work regularly inside classrooms for this to occur. If teachers enjoy this kind of contact, then they should certainly have the opportunity to put it into practice. If they feel uncomfortable with it, it is difficult to justify any element of compulsion.

Whatever the school policy in relation to parents, they are a critical factor in each teacher's plans for the children in his class and the teacher who does not take full account of them ignores a very valuable source of support. There are very few parents who are not positively concerned about their children's progress and almost everyone will willingly co-operate in any scheme which involves his child. If a teacher intends to try a particular way of handling a child or if he has planned a specific series of tasks for him, it is an obvious first step to explain this to the parent and ask for his support at home. This may simply require moral backing or may involve him in giving help with a learning task. In either case, once he understands what the situation is the parent is most likely to play his part to the immense benefit of the child.

Non-teaching adults in the school, whether their relationship to the children is personal or professional, can undoubtedly play a part of some importance in either facilitating or impeding the development of understanding between teachers and children in primary schools. Whether or not they enter into a partnership with teachers depends very largely on the initiative of the professional teaching staff of the school. If they regard non-teaching adults as a potential source of disturbance to the smooth running of the school, then this is what they may very well be. If, on the other hand, they look upon them as a possible source of assistance and support, then opportunities can be made for them to develop such a role.

Chapter 10

Outside the Classroom

Once children are outside the classroom they become part of a wider community and potentially subject to many more sources of control than their classroom teacher. If these sources of control are co-ordinated into a common policy, then the conventions established within the classroom will be reinforced and extended in the wider context of the school. If they operate idiosyncratically or fail to operate at all, then the conventions of the classroom will be challenged and even negated. Whether the situation is one of conflict and confusion or stimulus and reassurance is largely a matter of how the headteacher runs the school and how the staff relate to each other as a team. If there is no evident overall policy for how children should behave around the school, then no one could blame them for taking advantage of every opportunity to behave as the mood takes them. If teachers appear to confine their attention to their own class and show no interest in the concerns of children from other groups or teachers of other classes, then it will not be surprising if children's loyalties begin and end in their own classroom.

THE SCHOOL CONTEXT

Many of the principles which govern good control inside a classroom apply equally well to control throughout the school. The need is for conventions to be established which are reasonable and which everyone understands and subscribes to. There are places where you can run and places where you must walk. There are times when you can talk and times when you must be silent. There are rooms which you can enter freely and rooms where you must knock. More importantly, there are ways of treating people which are acceptable and others, like bullying, which are definitely not.

Rules like these are a perennial part of school life so that the establishment of them is not developmental as within a classroom. They are there when each newcomer joins and he quickly learns them. From time to time, of course, the community needs to be reminded of them and attention may then be focused on a particular convention for a while, but in the main, they are a permanent feature of school life.

The source of such conventions is the headteacher, in consultation, to a greater or lesser degree depending on his style of management, with the staff as a whole. The responsibility for ensuring their maintenance rests with every adult in the school. If teachers ignore those children who are not their immediate responsibility, this leaves the headteacher with the impossible task of attempting to maintain standards of behaviour throughout the school. Worse still, the children are left with the impression that a teacher's care is strictly of twelve months' duration, not beginning until they join his class and ending promptly in July.

Where teachers accept every child in the school as their responsibility, then every situation that calls for attention receives it. This means that no infringement is left unremarked and every misdemeanour is somehow followed up, so that the scope for flouting conventions is drastically reduced. At the same time, the scope for remaining without help when it is needed is also drastically reduced for teachers show interest in the concerns of all children they come across.

Corporate responsibility does not, of course, mean that every member of staff submerges his identity within a sort of common persona. This would be impoverishing to the children who have so much to gain from the differences in personality, outlook and interests which are present in every staff team. But enlivening differences of this kind do not prevent a group of individuals from agreeing a set of values and a common purpose which can form the basis of a policy which they will combine to put into effect.

Such a policy will influence children's behaviour in a general way as they move about the school and provide an overall setting for classroom behaviour. But school-wide behaviour itself occurs in a setting. The physical environment and the activity in which children are involved are both important parts of the context for this behaviour. The physical environment incorporates all parts of the school beyond the immediate classroom and the activity is mainly centred round events of a routine nature such as school assemblies, playtime and dinner-time and those which are special like concerts and plays.

THE PHYSICAL ENVIRONMENT

It has been argued that the environment inside a classroom has an important effect on the children who work there. Equally, the environment throughout the school cannot but be influential on the attitudes and manner of behaving of the children generally. If you are required to take care of the things in your own room but not in the school as a whole, then it must mean that the wider community is not very important. If your teacher takes pride in making your own room attractive but does nothing for the common areas of the school, then he must think that it is not worth bothering with the world outside your home-base. If the headteacher never provides anything to attract your interest and attention around the school, then he probably cares little about you or what you think. It is difficult for children to escape such conclusions and even if they are unable to give voice to them, they can certainly act in accordance with them.

Barren corridors, untidy libraries, dog-eared notices, isolated pictures on faded paper, half-full milk bottles marooned on shelves, cascading piles of books with turned-up corners, dead or dying plants – all these sights speak volumes to the casual visitor. To the resident, they must shout a message even more clearly. Outside the classroom is no man's land. Inside, it's the luck of the draw: sometimes you get a good year, sometimes not.

The school where there is a sense of corporate identity, where everyone has a positive sense of belonging, not just to a class but to the institution as a whole, tends to declare this from its physical appearance. Of course, the physical appearance *can* be there without the spirit but this is unlikely. It is such a lot of trouble to go to if you do not plan to take advantage of the opportunity it offers.

ROUTINE EVENTS

Assemblies

For most schools, assemblies are the most formal event of the day. This is partly due to the nature of the occasion itself: it is a semi-public event, often with religious significance, and many schools take the opportunity to give children the experience of being part of a suitably dignified procedure. It is also partly due to the fact that it would not be possible effectively to gather together what may be two hundred or more individuals in one space and then get them to behave with a degree of unity unless certain formalities governed the event.

No one set of formalities is innately superior to another. It is simply that formalities have to exist to co-ordinate the behaviour of so many people and those that do should reinforce each other and take account of what is possible and what they have been set up to achieve. The danger is that the formalities may conflict with each other or may be too difficult in practice to observe.

If the assembly is to be a very dignified affair, for example, it would be better for everyone to sit and wait for it in silence rather than to chat. If everyone is waiting in silence, it would be better for classes to approach the hall quietly rather than in mid conversational flow. If the journey to the hall is such that it will be difficult for a teacher to check conversation once it has started, then it would be better to begin and maintain a very low key approach. The system arises naturally once priorities and practicalities have been examined.

There is also a need for agreed conventions to govern the conduct of any corporate activity once the assembly is actually under way. Nothing is more guaranteed to throw the whole procedure into chaos, for example, than a new pianist who plays through the whole verse of a hymn instead of just the first line, or who does not give a single note as a starting signal. Again, no one convention is right but the need for a convention is undeniable.

Nevertheless, not everything is relative. There are certain formalities which could be considered to be universally appropriate. It would be difficult to see any corporate event gaining from a disordered start, for example, and perhaps there should be an insistence that all children should approach assembly well controlled and in good order. This requires particular supervisory effort from staff for failure in this area is public.

The very formality of most school assemblies underlines the authority of the person, usually the headteacher, who is taking the event. Quite apart from the fact that he does most of the talking, the physical set-up usually reinforces this impression. Whether he stands or whether he sits, he will tend to be at a higher level than the children and he will face them on a one-to-many basis. There is no reason why this should not be so because it represents a reality in school relationships. But it is a pity if it is exclusively so because it is not the only reality of school relationships. Most schools would claim that every member of their society is important and corporate events can be made to demonstrate this from time to time.

There are endless ways in which the traditional headteacher-dominated school assembly can be varied. The most straightforward way is for other members of staff to take a turn if they wish or for the process to be split up into class or age-group assemblies led by a teacher with a particular responsibility in that area. Different members of staff are bound to have different ideas of how they want to conduct the events so that at the very least an element of variety is likely to be introduced.

More radical change arises from allowing the children themselves to be responsible for an assembly. Of course, a teacher has to be closely involved in the planning and production of such an event, but on the day itself, the children can take charge of the proceedings.

The simplest way of doing it is for a class at a time to be involved. Once they have chosen a theme, this can co-ordinate their work in many areas of the curriculum while they are preparing for the assembly. Much care will need to be taken over organisation and display of work and over how the theme can best be presented to the rest of the school on the day itself. It is usually possible to find a role in the presentation for every member of the class. A slow reader can often recite well; a shy child can speak in concert with other children; a child without linguistic gifts may be able to produce an excellent illustrative painting. Ways can be found so that everyone is able to identify with a purposeful class activity.

This kind of assembly is very hard work for the teacher who is ultimately responsible, behind the scenes, for the success of the event. The effort is worthwhile, however, for it provides experience for the children of working towards an end product and of public presentation which is valuable but not easy to devise in a normal school routine. For the school as a whole it provides novelty and an appreciation of other children's strengths and makes real the notion that they have an important part to play in school life.

Dinners

Dinners are a subject for contention in many primary schools. Teachers are not obliged to be involved and yet ultimately the headteacher remains responsible for the organisation of the meal-time. It is not surprising that newly appointed headteachers find themselves disproportionately preoccupied with school dinners or that any group of headteachers, however experienced, will talk about them indefinitely once the subject has been introduced.

There is undoubtedly a problem for teachers here. Those who have ever been part of a system where dinner duty meant patrolling, policeman-like, up and down rows of rowdy tables and along lines of bored children waiting to be served will remember what an unpleasant and impossible job they were required to do and will never voluntarily return to such an arrangement. On the other hand, it is difficult for us, as primary teachers, to claim an interest in the all-round development of the child and then to switch this off at midday and allow these same children to pass into another regime within the school where it may not be possible to maintain the same high standards of considerate and civilised behaviour that we set in the classroom.

Ultimately, each teacher has to decide for himself whether or not to play a part at meal-times. If enough teachers do agree to take part, then probably the least arduous and most rewarding system is family feeding where groups of children take their meals at small tables with a member of staff who serves them and chats to them as if they were a family at home. If the distribution system is well organised and older children play a part as fetchers and carriers, these arrangements are stress-free, provide good training for the children and enable teachers to consume a proper meal in much the same time as it would take them to eat sandwiches in the staff-room.

Unfortunately, family feeding requires a daily commitment of staff time and this might be difficult to achieve. It also requires the agreement of the local authority to provide daily free meals for all staff and not all authorities may be ready to give this nowadays. Alternatives must therefore be sought and the kind of systems that recommend themselves are those of the quick and easy to administer, that allow staff maximum influence for the minimum of effort. Even small adjustments to the system can improve matters: if first and second courses can be served from different places so that children can get their meals without too much queuing; if there is a good circulation system which keeps those returning plates away from those receiving meals; if there are permanent seats allocated so that troublesome combinations are avoided; in short, if waiting and scope for misbehaviour are cut to the minimum then dinner-time is likely to pass more smoothly and pleasantly for everyone. It then becomes more possible for a teacher to be effective and to demonstrate a continued concern for children without sacrificing too much time and effort in the dinner hour.

A further alternative, if the building, equipment and numbers allow, is to disperse arrangements for meals so that they are consumed in relatively small numbers at different points throughout the school. The principle, as with family feeding, would be, divide and civilise, and again the magnitude of the task is reduced for all those who take part.

The growing number of children who eat sandwiches at lunch-time has created a new problem in recent years. They can, of course, be simply absorbed into the general meal system or they can be dealt with separately. Much depends on how many are involved but some schools have worked out most successful arrangements where children simply eat their sandwiches in the room of whichever teacher has agreed to prepare for the afternoon in the early rather than the later section of lunch-time.

Whatever system is put into operation for dinners, it will get off to a smoother beginning if every teacher ensures that his children arrive at the starting-point in good order, even though this means a slight postponement of leisure on his part. No system which is really successful as opposed to one that just limps along can operate without some cost to teachers and only they can decide on whether the cost is worth the benefit. One of the things which might help them to come to a decision might be a series of visits to other schools at lunch-time for there is nothing quite so impressive to an outsider as a well-run, civilised meal-time, just as there is little that is as depressing as school meals that resemble feeding-time at the zoo.

Playtimes

Supervising the playground can only be considered a necessary chore. True there are insights to be gained from watching children play, particularly when these are children that you know well who are playing totally without reference to you. In a sense, it is rather like eavesdropping. But for the most part, watching other people have fun while you stand and shiver is not a very entertaining way of spending a quarter of an hour.

Nevertheless it has to be done, not only so that someone is there to deal with crises and to lend an ear to the disconsolate, but also so that general exuberance and boisterousness are kept within bounds. It would be nice to be able to say that at playtime all children can do just what they like but of course this is unrealistic as dangerous games may develop, windows may get broken and the playground may become a frightening place for the small or the timid. Ground rules based on consideration have to be made, therefore, and enforced just as anywhere else in the school. It is possible to keep these to the minimum if a school is fortunate enough to have more than one play area. One area can then be kept for younger children or for certain kinds of games, thus allowing greater freedom in the other, but few schools have this type of luxury.

The beginning of playtime is usually no problem except for the teacher on duty who has to remember to get himself out into the yard in time. If teachers are operating flexible systems of working in classrooms, then children will tend to drift into the yard a few at a time. If it is the custom for everyone to finish at the same time, then it is not arduous for the teacher to see the children into the yard at the beginning of playtime.

The end of playtime is more difficult. Children have to switch from the exuberant behaviour of the playground to the more controlled behaviour which is expected inside the school. For some it is not easy and much time may be wasted and many unfortunate incidents occur in this transition period unless there is adequate supervision of children. Unless the geographical layout of the school is exceptionally favourable, however, it is unlikely that the solitary teacher on duty can provide this supervision. There are various ways of bringing in help for this critical few minutes: the teacher on duty may send a message to the staff-room announcing the imminent end of playtime; teachers who are still in their rooms may have reciprocal agreements whereby they cover for each other; this may be a time when the headteacher and particularly the deputy headteacher are very much in evidence. No one solution is likely to be adequate but in conjunction they can work well.

Wet playtimes are every teacher's nightmare and it is difficult to see how they can be other than a trying experience if children are to be properly supervised. Leaving classes in rooms while the one teacher on duty patrols the building subjects the children to risk and is unlikely to prove a good preparation for the following period either for the teacher concerned or for the children. If all teachers stay with their children then nobody gets a break but at least a tranquil atmosphere is maintained and if the comic box is kept well supplied then the task is not too demanding for the teacher.

Perhaps as more schools acquire video-recorders, it will become possible to keep something on hand to show to the children at such times. In suitable conditions, it would then be feasible for one or two staff to supervise the whole school, particularly if the deputy head takes on the role of supporter at such times as part of his duties.

SPECIAL OCCASIONS

Public occasions such as concerts and plays which bring outsiders into the school can be very testing. Children are tempted to show off and teachers are often at a low ebb after days of feverish preparation. There is always an underlying fear that the children will behave badly and the whole event will collapse into chaos.

Essentially, though, the success or failure of the enterprise in terms of children's behaviour depends on the extent to which conventions are established in normal situations. Special occasions rely on the extension of those conventions into unusual circumstances. If children are used to listening considerately when someone is speaking, they will find it easier to keep quiet back-stage; if they are used to waiting ungrudgingly for their turn, they will find the waiting that is always part of such special events more tolerable; if they habitually move quietly about the school, they will be likely to approach the assembled audience quietly.

Special events can be excellent for promoting the image of the school and for bringing parents into the building. They can also serve another useful purpose, however, and this is in consolidating the relationship of a teacher with a class. In working towards a common end teacher and children are usually brought closer together and the final event itself can often be seen to join them in a bond of mutual appreciation and support in the presence of outsiders. This commitment is likely to endure when the event itself has faded in the memory. Perhaps there is a good case for holding such an event in the first term of every year.

OUTSIDE THE SCHOOL

When children move outside the school, they become subject to an even wider variety of control than in the school at large for they are no longer part of a closed community where they are easily observed and held accountable for their actions. They are operating in a far wider and looser context where the opportunities for getting away with things are greatly increased and where it may not be easy for a teacher to exercise sanctions. Indeed events outside the school are an acid test of relationships and the teacher's control of a class.

Outside trips may be regular occurrences, as with visits to the baths or local playing fields, or they may be exceptional events, such as visits to the theatre or summer-time excursions to the country or the seaside. Primary school children tend to respond, on these occasions, in one of two contrasting ways. They seem to transform themselves either into Rabble Road County Primary or into St Dominic's Academy for the Children of Gentlefolk.

As Rabble Road, they move either with great speed (for example, to the beach) or infuriating slowness (for example, getting dressed at the baths). In either case, the movement is accompanied by much noise and shouting. Lines are seldom made, or if made, not held longer than a moment, for temptations such as slot machines are not resisted and exhortations from the teacher rarely heeded. St Dominic's Academy stand open-mouthed at such displays: behaviour like that would be anathema! They move about quietly in well-ordered lines or groups, commenting in conversational tones on what they see, responding instantly to their teacher. They take a lively interest in their surroundings but are constantly aware of their group membership.

It is as if children move to the extreme of whatever way they usually behave so that a slight tendency to disorder becomes chaos and normal considerate behaviour reaches a standard which swells the hearts of their teachers with pride.

Again, much depends on the effectiveness with which conventions of behaviour have previously been established. If they are not already in operation, then public places are no place to learn them. If they are, then they can be extended to cover new ground such as is encountered on a trip outside school.

The other important element in a successful excursion is preparation, both of a general and of a specific nature. It is never too early to accustom children to experiences outside school. It may even pay to take them on walks in the neighbourhood with the main aim of training them in how to cross roads, how to behave in public, and so on. There is no reason why children should not learn quite specifically that because of the greater hazards and the greater need for consideration of others, even more rigorous standards of behaviour are required outside school. Regular visits such as those to the baths will also serve as preparation for special excursions.

Each special excursion does itself require special preparation, however, so that the full potential of the visit can be exploited, so that key activities such as eating and toileting are planned for and so that maximum periods of freedom are built in: however good the children are at conforming when required, the need for conformity is best kept to the minimum.

In the event, as with concerts and plays, it is the relationship between teacher and children that will count. If it is a case of banding together to show a good face to the outside world, then St Dominic's will win the day. If it is a case of children taking advantage of a teacher's vulnerability in public places, then Rabble Road will emerge triumphant.

References

Ashton, P., Kneen, P., Davies, F., and Holley, B. J. (1975), *The Aims of Primary Education* (London: Macmillan).

Bandura, A. (1969), *Principles of Behavior Modification* (New York: Holt, Rinehart & Winston).

Blenkin, G. M., and Kelly, A. V. (1981), *The Primary Curriculum* (London: Harper & Row).

Bowles, S. S., and Gintis, H. (1976), *Schooling in Capitalist America* (London: Routledge & Kegan Paul).

Boydell, D. (1978), *The Primary Teacher in Action* (London: Open Books).

Burstall, C. (1970), *French in the Primary School: Attitudes and Achievement* (Slough: NFER).

Burt, C., and Howard, M. (1952), 'The nature and causes of maladjustment among children of school age', *British Journal of Psychology*, Vol. 5, pp. 39–59. Also in P. Williams (ed.), *Behaviour Problems in Schools* (London: University of London Press, 1974), pp. 114-37.

Cane, B., and Smithers, J. (1971), *The Roots of Reading* (Windsor: NFER).

Central Advisory Council for Education (1967), *Children and their Primary Schools* (The Plowden Report), Vol. 1 (London: HMSO).

Clifford, M. M., and Walster, E. (1973), 'The effect of physical attractiveness on teacher expectations', *Sociology of Education*, Vol. 46, pp. 248–58.

Corrigan, P. (1979), *Schooling the Smash Street Kids* (London: Macmillan).

Cox, C. B., and Dyson, A. E. (1971), *The Black Papers on Education* (London: Davis-Poynter).

Cyster, R., Clift, P. S., and Battle, S. (1981), *Parental Involvement in Primary Schools* (Windsor: NFER).

Davie, R., Butler, N., and Goldstein, H. (1972), *From Birth to Seven* (London: Longman).

Dearden, R. F. (1976), *Problems in Primary Education* (London: Routledge & Kegan Paul).

Delamont, S. (1976), *Interaction in the Classroom* (London: Methuen).

Department of Education and Science (1970), *Reports on Education* No. 66: *Trends in School Design*, October 1970.

Department of Education and Science (1977), *Education in Schools* (Green Paper) (London: HMSO).

Department of Education and Science (1978), *Primary Education in England* (The Primary School Survey) (London: HMSO).
Department of Education and Science (1979), *Aspects of Secondary Education in England* (The Secondary School Survey) (London: HMSO).
Docking, J. W. (1980), *Control and Discipline in Schools* (London: Harper & Row).
Dunham, J. (1977), 'The effects of disruptive behaviour on teachers', *Educational Review*, Vol. 29, pp. 181-7.
Entwistle, H. (1970), *Child-Centred Education* (London: Methuen).
Flanders, N., and Havumaki, S. (1960), 'The effect of teacher-pupil contacts involving praise on the sociometric choices of students', *Journal of Educational Psychology*, Vol. 51, pp. 65-8.
Hamilton, D. (1977), *In Search of Structure* (London: Hodder & Stoughton).
Hannam, C., Smyth, P., and Stephenson, N. (1976), *The First Year of Teaching* (Harmondsworth: Penguin).
Hargreaves, D. H. (1967), *Social Relations in a Secondary School* (London: Routledge & Kegan Paul).
Hargreaves, D. H. (1972), *Interpersonal Relations and Education* (London: Routledge & Kegan Paul).
Hargreaves, D. H. (1976), 'Learning to be deviant in school: aspects of the hidden curriculum', in T. Roberts (ed.), *The Circumstance of Learning* (Manchester: Manchester University School of Education).
Hargreaves, D. H., Hester, S. K., and Mellor, F. J. (1975), *Deviance in Classrooms* (London: Routledge & Kegan Paul).
Hartley, D. (1978), 'Teachers' definitions of boys and girls: some consequences', *Research in Education*, Vol. 20, pp. 23-35.
Hartup, W. W. (1970), 'Peer interaction and social organisation', in P. H. Mussen (ed.), *Carmichael's Manual of Child Psychology* (3rd edn), Vol. 2 (New York: Wiley).
Heal, K. (1978), 'Misbehaviour among school children: the role of the school in strategies for prevention', *Policy and Politics*, Vol. 6, pp. 321-32.
Jackson, P. (1968), *Life in Classrooms* (New York: Holt, Rinehart & Winston).
King, R. (1978), *All Things Bright and Beautiful?* (Chichester: Wiley).
Kounin, J. S. (1970), *Discipline and Group Management in Classrooms* (New York: Holt, Rinehart & Winston).
Kyriacou, C., and Sutcliffe, J. (1978), 'Teacher stress: prevalence, sources and symptoms', *British Journal of Educational Psychology*, Vol. 48, pp. 159-67.
Lewin, K., Lippitt, R., and White, R. K. (1939), 'Patterns of aggressive behavior in experimentally created "social climates"', *Journal of Social Psychology*, Vol. 10, pp. 271-99.
Mabey, C. (1981), 'Black British literacy: a study of reading attainment of London black children from 8 to 15 years', *Educational Research*, Vol. 23, pp. 83-95.
McPhail, P., Ungoed-Thomas, J. R., and Chapman, H. (1972), *Moral Education in the Secondary School* (London: Longman).
Mussen, P. H., Conger, J. J., and Kagan, J. (1974), *Child Development and Personality* (4th edn) (New York: Harper & Row).
Nash, B. C. (1981), 'The effects of classroom spatial organisation on four- and

five-year-old children's learning', *British Journal of Educational Psychology*, Vol. 51, pp. 144–55.

O'Leary, K. D., and O'Leary, S. G. (1972), *Classroom Management: The Successful Use of Behavior Modification* (New York: Pergamon).

Palardy, J. M. (1969), 'What teachers believe – what children achieve', *Elementary School Journal*, Vol. 69, pp. 370–4.

Peters, R. S. (1966), *Ethics and Education* (London: Allen & Unwin).

Pidgeon, D. A. (1970), *Expectation and Pupil Performance* (Slough: NFER).

Richardson, E. (1973), *The Teacher, the School and the Task of Management* (London: Heinemann).

Ridgway, L. (1976), *Task of the Teacher in the Primary School* (London: Ward Lock).

Rist, R. C. (1970), 'Student social class and teacher expectations: the self-fulfilling prophecy in ghetto education', *Harvard Educational Review*, Vol. 40, pp. 411–51.

Roberts, R. (1976), *A Ragged Schooling* (Manchester: Manchester University Press).

Root, J. (1977), 'The importance of peer groups', *Educational Research*, Vol. 20, pp. 22–5.

Rosen, C. (1967), 'All in the day's work', in J. Britton (ed.), *Talking and Writing* (London: Methuen).

Rosenthal, R., and Jacobson, L. (1968), *Pygmalion in the Classroom* (New York: Holt, Rinehart & Winston).

Rousseau, J. J. (1911), *Emile* (trans. by B. Foxley) (London: Dent).

Rutter, M., Maughan, B., Mortimore, P., and Ouston, J. (1979), *Fifteen Thousand Hours* (London: Open Books).

Sharp, R., and Green, A. (1975), *Education and Social Control* (London: Routledge & Kegan Paul).

Shepherd, M., Oppenheim, B., and Mitchell, S. (1971), *Childhood Behaviour and Mental Health* (London: University of London Press).

Sherif, M., White, J. B., and Harvey, O. J. (1955), 'Status in experimentally produced groups', *American Journal of Sociology*, Vol. 60, pp. 370–9.

Skinner, B. F. (1968), *The Technology of Teaching* (New York: Appleton-Century-Crofts).

Skinner, B. F. (1969), *Contingencies of Reinforcement* (New York: Appleton-Century-Crofts).

Staines, J. W. (1958), 'The self picture as a factor in the classroom', *British Journal of Educational Psychology*, Vol. 28, pp. 97–111.

Taylor, W. (1980), 'Family, school and society', in M. Croft, J. Raynor and L. Cohen (eds), *Linking Home and School* (3rd edn) (London: Harper & Row).

Wiseman, S. (1967), 'The Manchester survey', Appendix 9, in *Children and their Primary Schools* (The Plowden Report), Vol. 2 (London: HMSO).

Index